Miles Davis

Miles Davis

Brian Morton

HAUS PUBLISHING • LONDON

Originally published published in Great Britain in 2005 by
Haus Publishing Limited
26 Cadogan Court
London SW3 3BX

A CIP catalogue record for this book
is available from the British Library

ISBN 1-904341-79-9 (paperback)

Design Rick Fawcett and typeset in Garamond
Printed and bound by Graphicom in Vicenza, Italy

Front cover: Arena Images
Back cover: Getty Images

www.hauspublishing.com

Contents

To my darling Sarah . . .

. . . two abandoned Miles songs . . .

"I Love What We Make Together" and "Let's Fly Away"

. . . and for John Robert Morton . . .

. . . two more familiar titles . . .

"Shout" and "Shhh/Peaceful"

Miles Davis :   Introduction

There is a special class of artists for whom there exist no terms of critical reference larger than those articulated in the work itself, or in the artist's writings about it. Pablo Picasso is an obvious example, seemingly omnicompetent, and in every form and style from the naturalistic to the abstract. So is Karlheinz Stockhausen, creator of a vast operatic cosmology and a proportionately huge body of texts and interviews explaining its procedures and significance. So, in their very different ways, are three Americans.

Norman Mailer's career as novelist, essayist, film-maker, poet, gadfly and sensationalist is pulled together by a strange Manichean metaphysics largely of his own devising. If Mailer is the epitome of the "performing self", Andy Warhol seemed to negate every last shred of personality in art - often casually consigning work to others - and yet it is now virtually impossible to see any of the three defining forces of the modern world - the fetishised news image, advertising, celebrity - other than through his pale, photophobic eyes. And then there is John Cage, arguably one of the most important artistic catalysts of the 20th century, notorious for making silence not just a dramatic device in music, but the substance of music itself. How to explain Cage's work, or that of any of the others, in terms more expansive than his own?

At first glance, a jazz trumpeter does not seem to belong in this company, but the career of Miles Davis offers curious parallels with them all. To be sure, he never articulated any coherent philosophy, made few coherent statements about his work, and not a few misleading ones, and even rejected the terminology of jazz itself. And yet Miles's silences are as evocative as Cage's, whether the silences that greeted callow questions

Young Miles in 1947

about his aesthetic or the silences he built into music.

Like Warhol, Miles was often content to leave aspects of his creation to other hands, relying on other composers within his groups, leaning heavily on the arranging skills of Gil Evans, Paul Buckmaster and Marcus Miller, and during his most creative period handing over an unusual degree of musical responsibility to his producer and engineer Teo Macero. Like Warhol in his youth, Miles in later life became an obsessive doodler and sketcher, leaving behind a body of artwork that acquired a substantial posthumous reputation. When no less a figure than Jack Lang, the French culture minister dubbed him "the Picasso of jazz" he was thinking less of Miles's graphic skills than the sheer richness of his musical creativity which seemed to take a new direction with every passing year and every new record, embracing virtually every jazz form from the blues to abstraction, from the headlong virtuosity of bebop to the deceptive simplicity of contemporary pop. It took him into other areas as well. At the beginning of the 1970s - new decades almost invariably sparked new creative initiatives from Miles - he was listening closely to the music of Stockhausen, fascinated by chance similarities between his own bandleading philosophy and the German composer's intuitive approach, between Stockhausen's ambitious use of electronics and his own attempt to bring to jazz some of the furious electric energy of rock, funk and soul.

As to Norman Mailer, he inadvertently provided the keynote to Miles's creative life when he described his own ambition to "catch the Prince of Truth in the act of switching a style". Like Miles, Mailer has never been afraid of confrontation, with others and with his own shortcomings. He has taken huge creative risks, dared to write in the crudest popular form and with impenetrable obscurity. He is almost as well known for his marriages and love affairs as for his writing, a media obsession that, however understandable, has hampered appreciation of his work as much as a parallel obsession with Miles's personal style hampered understanding of his music. Unlike Miles, Mailer has aired his political views in public. Indeed, he has developed a vast philosophical - or cosmological - system involving God and the Devil in perpetual conflict, existential violence, mysticism, cancer and a creeping plague at the heart of modern life. However far-fetched it may sound, Miles played a small part in the creation of that mythos. Mailer's notorious essay "The White Negro", his manifesto for the hipster-outsider who might shake the grey consensus of 1950s, was largely inspired by the fierce, separatist aesthetic of the beboppers.

There was also a personal connection between Miles and Norman Mailer. Aware that his (fourth) wife Beverly Bentley had had a relationship with Miles, possibly ongoing, Mailer put a version of him in a novel. Published in 1965, *An American Dream* is not just written in an edgy new style, but was produced in a risky new way, familiar to Charles Dickens but unthinkable in 20th century publishing, with each chapter published in a magazine before the next was written, offering no chance to correct false narrative trails. There's an obvious parallel with the new recording methods Miles was to pioneer later in the decade. His identity is disguised in that Shago Martin is a singer, not a trumpet player, but there is no mistaking the source. At the publication party, Miles came over and caressed Beverly's hair. There was an angry stand-off, two small pugilistic men with reputations and sexual egos out of all proportion to their actual stature. It was Norman Mailer who eventually backed down . . .In life, and in afterlife, Miles Davis answers to no logic but his own.

What follows is a plain narrative of a creative life. One hears very little in it from Miles himself because he left few published writings beyond laconic liner notes for records and because his *Autobiography*, ghost-written by poet Quincy Troupe, is as notoriously unreliable as Billie Holiday's *Lady Sings the Blues*. Over the years, I have spoken to many of those who worked with Miles, including drummer Jimmy Cobb, saxophonist Kenny Garrett, pianist Herbie Hancock, bassist Dave Holland, pianist Keith Jarrett, guitarist John McLaughlin, bassist Marcus Miller, keyboard player Joe Zawinul. I have chosen to quote from those interviews very sparingly indeed. Everyone who has ever worked with Miles remembers him with a curious mixture of deep affection and deeper ambivalence. Interviewees rarely give more than anecdotal impression of his working methods, and those stories are available elsewhere. By and large, their comments are aimed at redressing one or another misconception about Miles's character. He emerges here through his public actions rather than the words of others, and emerges as a flawed, complex individual with the ability of a perverse chameleon to change his temperamental colouration so that it *failed* to fit the mood of a given situation. If someone complimented or praised Miles, as conductor Quincy Jones did on Miles's farewell, retrospective night at the Montreux Jazz Festival in 1991, they were treated to his signature "F***　you". If someone challenged him, or persisted in their own stance and individuality, they were treated with warmth and respect.

I spoke to Miles twice, in 1985 and 1986, in London and in Glasgow and somewhat by accident. On neither occasion did we talk about jazz, fulfilling a hard-won journalistic reputation for coming back with the story, but the wrong story. We spent an hour in London talking about boxers, and somewhat longer in Glasgow talking about art, as Miles filled page after page with drawings. The only music we talked about was the sound of the Scottish bagpipes, which he declared to be "cool".

In *An American Dream* Shago Martin is Stephen Rojack's rival for the blond singer Cherry Melanie. There is already actual murder in the air when they meet, but for all his guilt and existential dread Rojack - or his creator - is able to give the best summing-up of Miles Davis yet written, albeit prefaced with a dismissive gesture.

"Actually, I did not enjoy him altogether. His talent was too extreme . . . he gave you a world of odd wild cries, and imprisoned it to something complex in his style, some irony, some sense of control, some sense of the way everything is brought back at last under control. And he had a beat which went right through your ear into your body, it was cruel, it was perfect, it gave promise of teaching a paralytic to walk . . . Shago Martin's beat was always harder, faster, or a hesitation slower than the reflex of your ear, but you were glowing when he was done, the ear felt good, you had been dominated by a champion . . ." The Miles Davis effect in a hundred words. The story of the life takes a little longer.

...that was the sound...

In 1950, a record came out called *Birth of the Cool*. It's a title that makes some claim to innovation. The name printed below it on the record sleeve implies a claim to authorship which as we'll see is equally questionable, but on the same subject one track listing and credit offers a fascinating biographical titbit. To jazz initiates a title like "Boplicity" would have suggested another of those fast, fiery, virtuosic themes - "Anthropology", "Ornithology" - which half a decade earlier had helped to define the style known as bebop or bop. They might have expected to hear a melody based on the chords of a standard Broadway tune - "I Got Rhythm" most probably, or possibly "How High The Moon", "Cherokee" or "Embraceable You" - but played at lightning speed by an orthodox modern jazz combo: trumpet, saxophone, piano, bass and drums.

What they'd have heard instead was on the surface very different. For a start, a larger group is playing, not quite a big band but certainly not the quintet format which Charlie Parker and Dizzy Gillespie had made the iconic vehicle of bop. Audible in the mix are trombone, French horn and tuba, and instead of the linear onrush of a Parker or Gillespie tune something altogether more complex in texture, slow and muted in delivery and with a less overt blues tonality.

An alert listener might have noticed that what was being billed as something new was actually a matter of presentation rather than substance. "Boplicity" and some of the other session material gathered together on *Birth of the Cool* were in fact bebop tunes interpreted in a more orchestral manner, with those familiar frantic horn and piano lines slowed down, broken up and distributed throughout a larger group. That same listener might, however, have noted that the tune was credited to someone who seemed to be new on the New York scene and wasn't known by reputation from the West Coast either. Cleo Henry wasn't in fact the composer at all, but the co-composer's mother.

Cleota Henry Davis was the wife of a successful East St Louis dentist. Raised like her husband in Arkansas, Cleo was two years his senior, born in 1900. They married shortly after Miles Dewey Davis II qualified at Northwestern University College of Dentistry, settling first in Alton, Illinois, where their first two children were born before moving to a prosperous and largely white neighbourhood district of East St Louis. There a second boy was born. By his elder son and namesake's account Miles Davis II was an irascible and impatient man, but also thoughtful and highly intelligent. In addition to his vocational qualification from Northwestern University Dental School, he was also a graduate of Arkansas Baptist College and Lincoln College, Pennsylvania, where the future Ghanaian president Kwame Nkrumah was a classmate, and was a profound believer in the principles of black self-determination set out by Marcus Garvey. Miles Davis II also stood - unsuccessfully - as State Representative for Illinois. His elder brother had studied at Harvard and in Europe and was for a time editor of a magazine called *Color*.

Cleo Davis was not an intellectual, but she was beautiful and cultured, "very glamorous . . . always dressed to kill" in her elder son's recall. Miles III's mother played violin, though it appears he was unaware of her other skill as a blues pianist until some years after he left the family home; it's probable that his musicality, like his slight but powerful frame, came from the Davises, who back in slavery days had entertained plantation owners with recitals of classical music. Nonetheless his pride in his mother was intense. When in later years Miles Davis was attending a prestigious awards dinner at the White House, he rounded savagely on a white woman who commented that his "mammy" would be very proud of him.

That may suggest a warmer and more loving relationship than actually existed. Miles may have taken his looks - dark-skinned but with an almost East Indian strain - and his sense of style from his mother but they were

Miles and his trumpet. c1958

too tempestuously similar in personality to be close. Given the shaky nature of the Davises' marriage - they eventually divorced - it may be that she recognised too many of her husband's traits in the boy. Whatever the reason, though, at a point in his life when he had successfully declared independence from his family and set aside his father's ambitions for him as a classical musician - the Davises had apparently played chamber music for their masters during the slavery days - he attributed one of his most distinctive early compositions to her. Perhaps "Boplicity" was based on a theme he remembered her playing, or perhaps the version given in his ghosted autobiography *Miles* - that he and co-writer Gil Evans had simply wanted to publish the tune with another publishing house to the one he was contracted to - is true. (Some of the things said in *Miles* patently aren't.) The use of his mother's maiden name may be a mere practicality or it may be a sign of solidarity against the father whose wishes he had flouted. Whatever the case, it remains a complex gesture.

Miles Dewey Davis III was born in Alton on May 26 1926. His sister Dorothy was two years older; Vernon was born in the year of the Wall St Crash. As the middle child, Miles seems to have been less indulged than his younger brother, who later came out as a gay man, but looked to his older sister for encouragement and support. His small stature is evident in family photographs. Even so, when his mother and father separated, considerable responsibility fell on the teenager, arguably honing the formidable organisational skills he showed through most of his career.

It was clear from an early age that the only thing Miles - or Junior - wanted to do was play music, and specifically the trumpet. He was loaned his first instrument by a medical colleague of his father's, a Dr Eubank, and subsequently began to take lessons from one of Miles II's patients and drinking friends, Elwood Buchanan, who taught band at Lincoln High School. Presumably to consolidate the influence, Miles was transferred from Attucks Junior High to Lincoln, which had both junior and senior sections. Buchanan deserves a small footnote in jazz history since it was apparently he who persuaded the young Miles to play clean, vibratoless notes - the so-called "St Louis Sound" associated with men like Harold "Shorty" Baker - in contrast to the falsely dramatic wobble of many of the white players. Buchanan was also a friend of another trumpeter (and, almost as important for Miles, boxing fan) Clark Terry, who became one of the young man's most important sponsors and helped open him up to the music scene in St Louis, just across the Mississippi River in the state of Missouri.

Buchanan's coaching wasn't the only early lesson in the racial colouration of music. On Miles's 13th birthday, over and above his mother's wish that he should learn the violin, Miles sr bought him a new trumpet of his own. As Ian Carr points out in his biography, the respective choice of instrument was not just a domestic flashpoint, or reflective of individual tastes, but symbolic of deeper social imperatives. Neither parent was happy when Miles proposed to leave high school early to go on the road with Tiny Bradshaw, but for rather different reasons. Roles might later have been reversed, but for the moment while Cleo Davis craved acceptance by her white neighbours - hence her insistence on a respectably "classical" instrument - her husband took self-conscious pride in his black heritage, and may in addition have been reacting against his family's cultural servitude back in Arkansas, playing Strauss waltzes for white folks.

Arkansas was to play a role in Miles jr's musical upbringing as well. He and his siblings spent a considerable amount of time with their grandparents, uncles, aunts and cousins there, visits that would involve visits to prayer meetings far more unfettered musically than the polite services the Davises attended in East St Louis. In addition to hot gospel, Miles would have been exposed to the blues and fieldsongs. His education in swing was initially through the radio, in particular a show called *Harlem Rhythms*, which played a mixture of classic blues, hot jazz and contemporary big band arrangements; Miles apparently heard the programme once and decided on the spot that "*that was the sound*".

Perhaps unexpectedly, given her ambition that her children should partake in mainstream white culture and not what was still called "race music", Cleo also bought her son records by Duke Ellington and Art Tatum. Of such gifts, much can come and a decade later Miles might well have been paying back a complex musical as well as emotional debt.

Birth of the Cool is a key document in Miles Davis's emergence as an artist, and not just because it offers a whiff of family romance. Quibbles about its exact attribution have tended to obscure awareness about what

Duke Ellington was an important early influence for Miles Davis

kind of record it is. Casual looks at the instrumentation and personnel have muddied the picture still further. It is clear that many hands were involved in the project. When Miles aired his nonet at the Royal Roost club in the late summer of 1948, during a union ban that forbade recording, it was clearly flagged "Arrangements by Gerry Mulligan, Gil Evans and

John Lewis". And yet the eventual record, issued on Capitol once union restrictions had been lifted, was released under Miles's name only. After the trumpeter's death in 1991, there was a brief flurry of rival claims, not least from baritone saxophonist, composer and arranger Mulligan who suggested he merited an equal share in the credit.

The facts are that *Birth of the Cool* was what Miles himself called "a collaborative experiment", drawing ideas from many sources, but that it was Miles alone who acted as what old band musicians would have recognised as the "straw boss", hiring rooms, booking rehearsal time, phoning musicians and ultimately dealing with Capitol.

The nature of the music is initially more contentious. The presence of white musicians like Mulligan, alto saxophonist Lee Konitz and trombonist Mike Zwerin led some to complain that Miles was being less than loyal to fellow African-Americans at a time when work was scarce. Mulligan was later to be closely associated with trumpeter Chet Baker - known as "the white Miles Davis" - whose angular good looks and frat boy clothes, though at odds with a lifelong drug habit, became for fans a more potent signifier of "Cool" than anything in the actual music.

Miles recognised that a few white faces in the band and a few hummable tunes on the album would win over white audiences who had been alienated by the fiercely separatist ethos of bebop - devised, according to one paranoid scenario, specifically to keep out hip "ofays" who believed they could keep pace with Negro jazzmen - but it would be a major category error to think that *Birth of the Cool* in any way represented a whitening of his musical approach, or indeed that Miles Davis ever turned his back on his most personal and profound musical heritage. He takes pains in his autobiography to insist that *Birth* "came from black musical roots", from the work of Duke Ellington and Billy Strayhorn, from Fletcher Henderson and from Gil Evans' former employer Claude Thornhill. In insisting on that lineage and on a certain sweetness and communicability in his music, Miles was simultaneously confirming and distancing himself from his most important professional debt and from the style of music he had learned to play with Charlie "Yardbird" Parker.

. . . too white for me . . .

One of the many unexamined generalisations that have attached themselves to Miles Davis is that he was only an unwilling and uncomfortable exponent of bebop. There are certainly moments in his early recording career where his technique seems unequal to the ultra-fast articulation and harmonic sophistication associated with the style, but such errors are to be found in the work of most of the other major boppers - Charlie Parker perhaps excepted - and the bulk of evidence suggests that Miles was perfectly competent in the idiom.

Whether it represented his natural musical direction is another matter. Miles certainly evolved into a very different kind of player: spacious, textural, often minimalist; but even in later years, when he was pursuing the dark, volcanic abstraction of records like *Agharta* and *Pangaea,* and even at the end of his life when he was once again exploring the blues, there is a constant thread of bebop sensibility in his playing.

Even to attempt an estimate of Miles's place in this dramatic new idiom requires some understanding of what bebop, rebop or just bop actually was and where it came from. There is a tendency, even among otherwise astute jazz historians, to characterise the emergence of bebop as a revolution in the music. As a result, musical conservatives often define themselves by their attitude to it. Partly because the idiom emerged during wartime and during a union recording ban that meant its early stages weren't fully documented, its exact origins remain obscure. It was, though, an evolution and a development out of orthodox swing rather than a genuinely new style. The consensus is still that bebop emerged out of jam sessions in Harlem, at clubs like Minton's where proprietor Teddy Hill was happy to flout a union prohibition against unpaid performance. As jams progressed, successive

Charlie Parker and Max Roach at a jukebox, Los Angeles. 1954

soloists would move further and further away from the melodic structure of a song, improvising on its chords only, but often changing them radically, using wider intervals. Bop players often flatted the fifth note of a chord, a technique that created unexpected back passages from one key to another. Most bebop "compositions" are actually "contrefacts", radical reworkings of the chord structure of standard songs, very often "I Got Rhythm", but also "Cherokee", "How High The Moon", "Embraceable You" and others. Players started to use phrases of unusual, irregular lengths, often delivered at competitively high speeds. Syncopation was largely abandoned. creating a tough, rebarbative style in which cleverness was often an end in itself, though its other presumed end, when matched in conversation by impenetrable "hipster" argot and tune titles like "Klactoveesedstene", was to shut out less sophisticated hangers-on, slumming white dancers and, significantly, out of towners. In some quarters, bebop was seen as New York jazz putting out its elbows to the rest of the country.

In reality, it is clear that bebop is a classic instance of simultaneous evolution, its apparently sudden appearance on the scene a matter of happenstance rather than a quality of the music itself. It also represents jazz's development away from entertainment (almost invariable white-controlled) and in the direction of self-determined art. It's evident that older players like trumpeter Roy Eldridge, guitarist Charlie Christian and above all saxophonist Lester Young (also a pioneer of bizarre hipster slang) were all dabbling with elements of the bebop style before the war. There was a geographical dimension, too. Miles Davis was always insistent that he heard Mid-West players like Kansas City trumpeter Buddy Anderson working in at least a proto-bop style long before he heard Charlie Parker or Dizzy Gillespie either in person or on record. It would have been some time before he could have heard either of them on radio, either. Though it quickly became an irresistible market force, bop wasn't universally welcomed. Even the great Cab Calloway, a man of shrewd commercial judgement, dismissed it as "Chinese music", a description perhaps lent some weight by the pseudonym Charlie Parker used when playing on a non-contractual session: "Charlie Chan". In a period before Black Power and concepts of *negritude*, the new style's "African" characteristics, though more accurately identified, were also subject to suspicion and hostility.

Like all cultural mythologies, though, the emergence of bebop also has a creationist dimension. The catalytic moment is supposed to have been when Charlie Parker, playing "Cherokee" in a Harlem club, broke with normal practice and based his improvisation on the higher intervals of the chord instead of its root note, a practice that required the song's harmonic structure to be resolved differently. If such a moment actually occurred in the way Parker and his first biographers have described, it may have been more important to him personally than to the development of a style. The anecdote also creates the impression that bebop was born whole out of Charlie Parker's head, even though it is clear that some of the earliest recordings in the idiom, notably those on the Savoy label, are still tentative enough to be considered experimental.

These are potent and durable myths, suggesting that bebop was the invention of a small group of virtuoso horn and piano players and their disciples. Given that the front men continued to play fiery runs of 16th notes even over weirdly slow tempos, it was entirely predictable that outside observers might believe the rhythm sections were struggling to keep up. In fact, as often as not, the tail was wagging the dog. Right from the beginning of his career, Miles Davis instinctively understood that evolutions in jazz are almost always evolutions in the rhythm section rather than the front line. That was certainly true of bebop where drummers like Max Roach and Kenny Clarke devised a new approach to rhythm with the metre sounded on a hi-hat cymbal and punctuated by bomb-dropping accents on the formerly central bass drum. The role of bass players at the time is harder to assess since contemporary recordings rarely flattered them. Changes in Miles's own music were often signalled by the recruitment of radically different drummers and bassists, most notoriously the teenaged, and from some perspectives minimally talented, Michael Henderson in 1969 when Miles began to explore a new fusion of jazz and rock. Crude as he may have sounded compared to a Curly Russell, a Ron Carter or a Paul Chambers, Henderson became the anchor of some of Miles's most radical sessions.

It was saxophonist Sonny Stitt, the man saddled with a reputation as Charlie Parker's apostolic successor, who first dangled the possibility that Miles might have a role in the bebop "revolution". The teenager was playing with Eddie Randle's Blue Devils, a job he had gained partly through Clark Terry's sponsorship, partly because he had taken his girlfriend's dare and phoned Randle asking for an audition. At 19, Irene Birth (later Cawthon) was three years older than Miles, closely mirroring the age gap between his parents, and seems to have had a strong influence on him; she later joined Miles in New York, apparently with his mother's blessing, and they had three children, Cheryl and Gregory , and, somewhat later, Miles IV.

Her instinct was spot on. Randle employed Miles from the summer of 1943 to that of 1944, and seems to have used him as band director, rehearsing the musicians and preparing the "charts" or arrangements they played. Stitt, visiting town with Tiny Bradshaw's band and spotting Miles at the Rhumboogie Club, told him that he looked like "a man called Charlie Parker and you play like him too . . ." This is hard to believe on either count, and may have been no more than a tactic in the cut-throat world of band recruitment, especially when wartime military conscription had depleted personnels. "Bird" Parker - or Yardbird, after his passion for fried chicken - was already a pudgy, well-set man and already bound for greatness; Miles Davis was a skinny youngster, clearly determined and committed but hardly yet more than a competent technician whose jazz credentials were still tinged by his ongoing classical studies. Nevertheless, the comment must have seemed like an anointing. Miles became obsessed with Parker and when he moved to New York City in the autumn of 1944, ostensibly to continue his classical education, he spent much of his time and money seeking Parker out.

He was, in the meantime, receiving and mostly turning down offers of professional employment, mostly because they would have involved leaving home before high school graduation, which both parents forbade. He did, however, accept a local engagement - the Illinois state capital Springfield is just miles from East St Louis - with a visiting band from Louisiana, Adam Lambert's Six Brown Cats. He also saw Charlie Parker (and Dizzy Gillespie) for the first time when the Billy Eckstine band, universally known as "the Band", or "Mr B's Band", when they played an engagement at Club Riviera in St Louis. They arrived lacking a third trumpet player (ironically, it was his friend Buddy Anderson, who had been diagnosed with TB) and once Gillespie, acting as the group's "straw boss", had determined that Miles held a valid union card, he asked him to sit in.

Charles Mingus on bass, Roy Haynes on drums, Thelonius Monk at the piano and Charlie Parker in performance in New York. 1953

Versions vary. Miles claimed to know the band parts intimately, but Eckstine was sharply dismissive. What he learned musically in a fortnight can only be guessed at, but the experience of meeting the shrewd Gillespie was important and there is some evidence that Miles later based his blunt, forthright approach to hiring and firing, his tough boxer's style with promoters and label bosses, and some at least of his sense of style, on the deceptively languid and elegant Eckstine. When "the Band", with its lineaments of something new in jazz, moved on, Miles felt the void and determined to renew his brief acquaintance with Bird and Diz.

In September 1944, the 18 year old Miles enrolled at the Juilliard School of Music in New York City. He roomed with family friends from East St Louis; his father paid the fees and board and gave Miles an allowance. It was quickly spent, as Miles scoured the clubs of Harlem and 52nd Street (the commercial centre of bebop, if not its cradle) looking for Charlie Parker.

He says little in his autobiography about Juilliard except that "The shit they was talking about was too white for me". Miles spent his days studying theory and playing in the school orchestra - two notes every ninety bars was unlikely to satisfy a youngster who'd already played with the Eckstine band - and his nights standing out personally if not yet musically on the jazz scene: well-dressed, well supplied with cash - he could even afford horseback riding at uptown stables - quietly self-possessed and apparently obsessed with Charlie Parker. Miles renewed contact with Dizzy Gillespie, who welcomed him into his home, and eventually met his idol as well.

For anyone else, the reality of Parker, who tapped Miles on the shoulder one night at the Heatwave club, would have been disillusioning. Though later he would develop a serious drug habit, at this stage in his life Miles was "clean" and sober. Parker was anything but. Addicted to heroin, dexedrine, marijuana, nutmeg, alcohol and food, the 24 year old was an unprepossessing sight, except when he played music, which he did with consummate skill no matter what his physical condition.

Miles's hero-worship was undented. For Parker, the unquestioning friendship of a young man with plenty of money brought obvious benefits. What he thought of his musical abilities is less clear. Miles played with Parker on a number of occasions, though, by his own admission, he did little more than follow the leader and fill out the sound; one hears him doing this on his first recording session with

Parker, on "Billie's Bounce", where his apprentice status is further underlined by a glaring wrong note in the closing ensemble. Parker also returned favours in informal tuition and by introducing Miles to other pioneering bebop musicians, notably pianists Thelonious Monk, whose virtuosic use of space made a lasting impact, and the hugely underrated Tadd Dameron, whose elegant compositions and arrangements are a less fully acknowledged influence. Miles also caught the eye of tenor saxophonist Coleman Hawkins, acknowledged as one of the greatest improvisers in the history of the music, who like Parker seemed to see something beyond the young man's lack of natural affinity for the blues and beyond the slightly stiff "classical" harmony he was unwillingly imbibing at Juilliard.

Miles didn't return to classes at the beginning of the autumn 1945 semester. He returned home to St Louis to explain the situation to his father, who accepted the situation readily enough, agreed to continue Miles's allowance and advised him to be his own man musically. Cleo Davis was presumably less pleased. By this time, Miles had some hopes of carving out a career around 52nd Street. He'd been hired by another tenor player Eddie Lockjaw Davis (no relation) at the Spotlite club, his first formal engagement in New York, and with Charlie Parker at the Three Deuces. On April 24 1945 (Carr states May 4), he took part in his first recording session, with saxophonist Herbie Fields and singer Rubberlegs Williams; though what was to become his distinctive muted sound is already evident in embryo, Miles took a relatively modest part in the proceedings - "no solos", he noted laconically.

There was nowhere to hide on his next visit to the studios, however. On November 26 1945, a date modern jazz fans can reel off as quickly as that of the Kennedy assassination, Charlie Parker fulfilled an engagement for Savoy records, one of the very few labels to show an early interest in the new idiom of bebop; a trundling bandwagon would soon follow the lead. Savoy's later billing of the date as "the greatest recording session in modern jazz history" owed much to hindsight, but it is ironic given Miles's reputation as an uneasy bebopper that he should have been

Miles is on the right, playing with Charlie Parker and Tommy Potter at the Three Deuces in New York. 1947

present at this pioneering session. Also present were, of course, Parker, bassist Curly Russell and drummer Max Roach; the pianist should have been Thelonious Monk, but he didn't show up, and was replaced at the last minute by Dizzy Gillespie, a competent and (like Monk) a quirky keyboard player, and on some of the faster tunes by Argonne Thornton, also known as Sadik Hakim. The fact that Gillespie's piano skills didn't stretch to soloing threw additional pressure on the two horn players.

Miles's still limited skills meant that he didn't play the twisting, difficult "Koko", which featured Gillespie - identified on the original release by the *nom de session* Hen Gates - and a stunning solo from Parker, who built the theme on the chords of "Cherokee".

Apart from "Billie's Bounce", Miles only played on two other tracks at the session. Notwithstanding the hash he once again makes of the closing ensemble, "Thriving on a Riff" represents his first successful recorded solo. Miles plays with a cup mute - rather than the modified Harmon mute that defined his later sound - and phrases very elegantly, perhaps a little prissily. He also plays twenty four solo measures on "Now's The Time", a statement that contrasts sharply with Parker's blues-tinged feature. Much of Miles's later development can be heard here in embryo: a preference for middle-register playing rather than the skyscraping high notes favoured by jazz trumpeters from Louis Armstrong to Roy Eldridge and Hot Lips Page, to Dizzy Gillespie; great economy of means, with few decorative grace notes; a rich ambiguity in the harmonics; and a certain bittersweet edge to the playing which suits the twilit nature of the piece better than it does "Billie's Bounce".

The two tracks were released together as opposite sides of a 78 r.p.m. disc. They confirmed Parker's extraordinary talent, but they also introduced Miles to a wider audience and established his reputation (among musicians, if not initially among the critics) as a player whose flawed technique was matched by a distinctive originality of approach. If newspaper journalists likened him negatively to Dizzy Gillespie, those really in the know recognised Miles's debt to his friend Freddie Webster, though he couldn't yet combine Webster's uncluttered, emphatic approach - again characteristic of the "St Louis sound" - with pin-sharp accuracy.

(In fairness, it should be added that even Parker's playing is not absolutely pristine. In 1945, tracks had to be recorded in a single take, without internal editing, hence the plethora of "breakdowns" and discarded takes that bulk out the discography. Even on the released takes, though, Bird makes mistakes, and sounds as if he is playing with a damaged saxophone reed, testimony, perhaps, to the relatively casual attitude most musicians held toward recording, still in those days far less important in career terms than live appearance.)

Miles returned to East St Louis as a recording artist with a growing reputation and as a father. There is no doubt which role meant more to him. Irene was pregnant with Gregory at Christmas 1945; he and Cheryl were to see little of their father as they grew up. The return to the Mid-West wasn't entirely sentimental. The New York police had purged 52nd Street in a clampdown on narcotics, and while this represented no personal threat to Miles Davis at this juncture, it did threaten to compromise his work schedule. Charlie Parker and Dizzy Gillespie (who was still for the moment Bird's trumpeter of choice) had moved to the more liberal West Coast and it was inevitable that Miles would follow. His berth with trumpeter/ saxophonist Benny Carter's big band was more congenial as a travel ticket than it was musically and in Los Angeles Miles reproduced the pattern of his Juilliard days, playing formal arrangements with Carter as a "day job" and then hunting down Parker for late-night sessions.

Once again, Miles showed a genius for judging the propitious moment, even if the company of the increasingly erratic Parker didn't quite qualify as "the right place". In February 1946, the saxophonist parted company with Dizzy Gillespie, who flew home with the rest of the group; Bird, typically, had cashed in his plane ticket to buy heroin. Less than a month later, Miles was recorded on the fly with Parker's makeshift West Coast group at the soon-to-be-closed Finale club. What's immediately ironic is how much like Gillespie he sounds, playing more notes and at higher registers than on his Savoy debut. That impression was reinforced when on March 28 Parker took a larger than usual group - augmented by tenor saxophone and guitar - into the studios of new Californian label Dial.

The Parker "Dials" - as fans know them - don't flatter Miles, who sounds awkward and unswinging on the mostly uptempo material. His phrasing is less sophisticated and his elegance is compromised by hurry. His preference for order and control must also have been challenged by his leader's chaotic working and social habits which would eventually lead to Parker's catastrophic breakdown and institutionalisation at Camarillo

State Hospital. When this happened Miles was already - albeit temporarily - separated from Bird, who was working with Howard McGhee, another fine bop trumpeter and fellow-addict, but more importantly co-owner of the re-opened Finale. Parker's loyalty was usually contingent on money.

It was Miles, though, who was seen as the traitor - except by Bird himself - when he took the opportunity of a touring spot with the Billy Eckstine band to get out of California and back to the East Coast, by way of Chicago. Once back in New York, he worked with saxophonist Illinois Jacquet (with whom he'd once turned down employment) and with Dizzy Gillespie, who had formed a big band: Freddie Webster, Fats Navarro and the released - but far from recovered - Charlie Parker were all in the line-up. As a bandleader, Dizzy was not prepared to overlook Bird's lapses and fired him; Parker, on the other hand, showed no resentment at being abandoned in California.

On May 8 1947, Parker and Miles, with pianist Bud Powell, bassist Tommy Potter and drummer Max Roach, recorded another four sides for Savoy. It was to be a busy two years for the group, which, with some variations of personnel, returned to the studio (for Dial) on October 28, November 4 and December 17, with further dates for Savoy on December 21 and again on September 18 and 24, 1948, by which time Miles was already experimenting with the innovative "Birth of the Cool" ensemble. One of the May 8 1947 tracks, "Chasin' the Bird" (a loaded title by any measure) was the first to be released under Miles's own name and on August 14 1947, he recorded his first full session as leader. The Miles Davis All Stars replaced Powell (another erratic genius with drug and psychological problems) with the urbane John Lewis, who was to play an important part as pianist and arranger with the "Birth of the Cool" band.

Immediately evident from the first of these dates is that Miles is no longer a Dizzy Gillespie copyist. His solos are similar to that on "Now's The Time", texturally complex rather than virtuosic, favouring the middle register of his horn and with a tighter, more compressed sound. The date also included his first recorded composition, "Donna Lee" (usually attributed to Parker) on which he demonstrates conclusively that he was in command of the bebop idiom, even if his playing was not always equal to Parker's. The surviving takes of the tune show him in control of its fast, tricky chord changes. As Carr points out, the tune's symmetrical structure is strong evidence that Parker, who favoured irregular melodic patterns, was not the composer. Typically, Miles fared less well on the two blues-based compositions, "Cheryl" and "Buzzy", but he shows considerable subtlety in his solos.

The All Stars session of August 14 is unique and significant not just because it was Miles's formal debut as leader, but because of Parker's decision to record on a tenor saxophone rather than his usual alto. Despite the lower register, the playing is unmistakably Bird's, but the switch to tenor does change the overall dynamic of the group, emphasising Miles's leadership and underlining his increasing independence from Parker, partly for musical, largely for personal reasons. The saxophonist's chaotic behaviour was actually the indirect reason why Miles led the session (and perhaps why Bird played an unfamiliar horn) because it was discovered that Parker was still under contract to Savoy and thus not entitled to work for another label. It's a flawed session, marred by Miles's overwrought writing, but it again signals his preference for a more even and more delicately structured sound, marked out by densely packed harmonics; when the Miles Davis of 1947 attempted a twelve-bar blues, as he did on "Sippin' at Bells", its chordal progression is almost crowded.

The trumpeter's playing is, by contrast, almost laid-back and almost for the first time one can hear the lineaments of what became a familiar performing personality: elided, "cool", utterly confident. The confidence was justified. Though Miles was to work with Parker many times again - the final studio encounter was in January 1951 for Norman Granz's Verve/Mercury/Clef but there are tapes of a live encounter from Birdland (the club named after Parker) from the spring of 1953, two years before the saxophonist's death - he was now unmistakably his own man. Cynical though he may have been about critical recognition, the accolade of *Down Beat* magazine's "New Star on Trumpet" for 1946 was a significant measure of Miles's growing visibility.

Morpheus

Freddie Webster's death in 1949 from a dose of bad heroin should have been a warning, but having begun his professional career in admirable sobriety - albeit often in the presence of serious drug users, which may help explain his abstention - Miles began to develop a serious drug habit. It would dog him for the next five years. It says much for his strength of character that he should finally confront and overcome the problem on his own, albeit with support along the way from his father and from Clark Terry, but even before his addiction was made public, fellow musicians were astonished to learn that the normally self-possessed Miles had succumbed and indeed was living a marginal existence, borrowing, stealing and even, by his own admission, pimping girlfriends to feed his habit.

His descent had both a personal and a cultural dimension. Though Miles rarely expressed overtly political ideas and never espoused a systematic philosophy, he was always conscious of the broader context of his own situation. In Paris he had fulfilled the Existentialist stereotype of the hip, tough, taciturn black jazz musician. He met Jean-Paul Sartre and the jazz-obsessed Boris Vian and fell in love with the elegant *chanteuse* Juliette Greco, an affair that continued intermittently for some years, leading Miles to neglect Irene and his children. Every bit as important, he encountered some of the most enthusiastic audiences of his career so far, whose wild applause - audible on live recordings - induced him to take tightrope risks in his playing. Even his phrasing and tone sound different from the year before, abrasive and wide, as if the last vestiges of Juilliard propriety had been rubbed off.

Miles returned from the 1949 Jazz Fair to a disillusioning lack of work, though there was a chance at last to make studio recordings with his pioneering nonet. The previous year had seen a second recording ban imposed by the American Federation of Musicians, not lifted until December 15 1948. Savoy flouted it in September with a Charlie Parker session in which Miles took part, but for the most part his wider public exposure - and a first chance to hear the challenging new direction he and his arranger colleagues were exploring - was restricted to radio broadcasts from the Royal Roost club in New York City, a venue sometimes nicknamed the "Metropolitan Bopera". Parker's flurry of recording activity in 1947, much of which featured Miles, had been a bid to lay up material before the ban and created a false sense of what could be considered a normal quota of studio work. The ban is credited with bringing to an end the big band era; it also spelled trouble for the nonet, which thanks to the complex nature of the music and the multi-racial line-up of the ensemble, already started at a disadvantage. Miles was ripe for disillusion and thus ripe for whatever comfort was on hand.

He had dabbled with cocaine and heroin on the Eckstine tour in 1947, and had begun to drink alcohol and smoke cigarettes, but with no hint that he might slide into addiction. His fall was sudden, as shocked reports in the music press underline. It was, however, part of a wider problem.

The role of drugs in jazz is controversial and widely debated, but is also undeniable. The early jazzmen - even the paternal Louis Armstrong - were enthusiastic marijuana smokers, as tune titles like "Muggles" reflect. Not until 1937 was a Federal law passed against marijuana use. Heroin, by contrast, had been outlawed in 1924, as part of a raft of measures designed to strengthen the Harrison Narcotics Act of a decade earlier, but the sorry experience of Prohibition should have persuaded American lawmakers and enforcers that there was a strong inverse relationship between illegalisation and extent of use. Alcohol consumption actually doubled after the Volstead Act of 1919 and dramatically increased consumption of hard liquor rather than beer. Similarly, an FDA ban on LSD in 1962 led to skyrocketing increase in use, while a 1968 military clampdown on marijuana among troops in Vietnam led many soldiers to switch to heroin instead.

Narcotic use was also not unknown in early jazz - opium, but also coca

Miles Davis on the left in the All Stars of 1949

products - and its dramatic proliferation in the 1940s and 1950s follows a similar cultural and socioeconomic logic. Simple psychology plays a part. Cocaine and heroin use were part of a perverse freemasonry among touring musicians, a sign of insider (or outsider) status, resistance to authority and often of a fatal bravado. Quite literally fatal in a good many celebrated cases.

The heroic mythology attached to narcotic addiction is not a sufficient explanation, however, and is something of a rationalisation after the fact.

The reality was that, particularly after the United States entered the Second World War in December 1941 drugs became ever more plentiful and cheap, certainly cheaper than good quality alcohol. Few human societies have ever been so comprehensively and enthusistically medicated as that of post-war America. Use of non-prescription barbiturates increased by 800% in the twenty five years after 1942; consumption of mild proprietary tranquilisers like Miltown was widespread. Many reasons are adduced, but the most obvious is purely circumstantial. American combat soldiers and airmen were generously supplied with both painkilling morphia in case of wounds and performance-enhancing amphetamines to increase alertness, resolve and resistance to pain in battle situations. When the war ended, a huge surplus of drugs flooded an already receptive market. Miles Davis was only one of very many young musicians who, even without military experience, reaped the whirlwind.

It's tempting to suggest that Miles's new style - cool, detached, introspective, more static than bebop - owed something to his drug habit, but such speculations evaporate in the face of more straightforward musical and personal explanations. Only the strange "Morpheus" from his January 1951 session sounds at all like a sonic realisation of a drug-induced state. As so often in his life, Miles's creative needs were answered by circumstance. As he, like other musicians, cast about for a new style that would take him beyond the increasingly imitated, decreasingly inventive bebop idiom, he met Gil Evans. The Canadian was almost fifteen years older, self-taught and as easy with classical music as he was with jazz. Working with pianist Claude Thornhill's elegant orchestra (for whom he'd made an arrangement of Miles's "Donna Lee") had opened Evans's ears to fresh possibilities in jazz instrumentation. The tuba had originally been used as a rhythm instrument, its place supplanted by the string bass when bands ceased to march. It had rarely, if ever, been used to fill out the harmony of a jazz ensemble; tubist Bill Barber was a significant recruit. Neither was the French horn much used, and it was this latter instrument, originally played by Junior Collins, later by Sandi Siegelstein, which added the defining new sound to Miles's nonet.

The other signature sound was the alto saxophone of Lee Konitz, a white player whose approach was the opposite of Charlie Parker's, light, smooth, played without vibrato and with virtually no blues component. Add to that the baritone saxophone (and precocious arranging skills) of 21 year old

Oscar Pettiford and Miles Davis performing at Birdland. 1949

Gerry Mulligan, soon to be one of the pioneers of West Coast Jazz alongside trumpeter Chet Baker, who became known as the "white Miles Davis"; the twin trumpets of Red Rodney and John Carisi (the latter another fine composer/arranger); the subtle piano playing of John Lewis, later a pioneer of so-called "chamber jazz" with the Modern Jazz Quartet; and the low-toned trombone of Mike Zwerin, later a distinguished journalist.

After Miles's death in 1991, Mulligan and others tried to reclaim authorship of the ensemble's music, though the saxophonist did graciously concede that "Miles was the prime mover" and that his distinctive playing directly influenced the compositions and arrangements made for the group. Mulligan must also have been aware that his prominent billing as arranger was unprecedented in jazz.

The group appeared at the Royal Roost during the late summer of 1948. An "airshot" recording of a radio broadcast from September 4 catches the group, with Al McKibbon on bass, Max Roach on drums and with singer Kenny Hagood adding a vocal on "Why Do I Love You"; Miles was also featured on the same broadcast with a Charlie Parker All Stars. With some changes, the two groups were back at the Roost on September 18, and further recordings were made of that broadcast. The impression these give is slightly misleading. Given that in live performance, jazz soloists generally play longer features than they would in the studio, the music doesn't sound as tightly or formally arranged as it would the following January and April and then again in March 1950 when Miles took the reconstituted nonet into a New York studio to record twelve tracks for Capitol.

"Godchild", "Move (Mood)", Evans's reworking of "Moondreams" and "Hallucinations (Budo)" had all been performed during the Roost sessions, and the two different recordings of the latter three numbers offer some sense of how the music was evolving even over the space of a summer. For the studio recording, several new pieces were added: the staccato "Jeru" (Mulligan's nickname), "Venus de Milo", "Rouge", "Boplicity" and John Carisi's "Israel"; in March 1950, "Deception" and "Rocker", together with a definitive "Moon Dreams" and Hagood's feature "Darn That Dream", were added; the last of these, intended as a sop to audiences who wanted vocal music, has quietly been dropped from subsequent reissues. These were the fruits of Miles's first contract as a leader. Capitol had also signed pianist Tadd Dameron, with whose similarly constructed Big Ten Miles had acquired valuable experience in February 1948, and may have been perplexed to find that a corporate decision to jump on the bebop bandwagon had yielded such unexpectedly sober music. Their misgivings were anticipated by lukewarm audiences at the Royal Roost.

Birth of the Cool didn't appear on 12" LP until 1957 and nobody used that much-quoted, misleading title in 1949 and 1950. The tracks were originally issued, as were all jazz recordings at the time, as 78s. This clearly has a bearing on how the music was performed in studio, spare, almost formal, and with new limitations on how far a soloist could break free of the ensemble. Though some of Miles's later work with Gil Evans, classic albums like *Miles Ahead* and *Sketches of Spain* cast him in a *concertante* role over an orchestral arrangement, these brief pieces were more radical in their revision of roles. "Israel" is almost a classical piece, contrapuntal and complex and presciently similar to the so-called "Third Stream" movement which became voguish in the 1950s. As it had been in the genesis of bebop, Max Roach's slowed down and subtle percussion is a vital element in the *Birth of the Cool* sessions. Though Miles would revert for a time at least to a more orthodox approach, the rhythmic evolutions of 1949 and 50 would filter down through his work for the next three decades. Both Miles and Tadd Dameron singled out "Boplicity" as their favourite recording from the sessions, but "Godchild" is the outstanding statement from the trumpeter, who plays with a lot of air in his sound and with a new understanding of musical space and time.

Miles now sounded like no one but himself, able to tinge a phrase with enough vibrato to give it drama, to add swing by the subtlest means and to combine precision with intense expression. In terms of public awareness, he was still a satellite of Charlie Parker, and he recorded with Bird again in January 1951 and under his own leadership exactly two years later, when Parker was identified as "Charlie Chan"; creatively, though, Miles had moved beyond bebop and had begun to ask searching questions about the nature, structure and internal relationships of the jazz ensemble. He may have broken free of Parker musically, but there was still a toxic legacy from the relationship.

Blue Haze

The commercial failure of the nonet - admired by musicians, ignored by fans - and an ongoing dependency on heroin had disastrous consequences. Miles played very little during 1950 and 1951, doing pick-up work and earning a few dollars from transcribing. Inactivity can be disastrous for a trumpeter, who needs not just daily practice to maintain a proper embouchure but regular playing opportunities, and it's a further measure of Miles's iron resolve that he should have come through the period with his sound unscathed.

One admirer in a position to do something about the 24 year old's faltering career was Bob Weinstock, founder of the New Jazz and Prestige labels. Miles was offered a much-needed contract and on January 17, 1951, the same day he recorded the classic "Au Private", "She Rote", "K.C. Blues" and "Star Eyes" on a Charlier Parker date for Verve, Miles cut four tracks under his own name with a new sextet. It featured tenor saxophonist Sonny Rollins, one of Miles's closest friends during his period of addiction and destined to become one of the modern giants on the instrument. At this point in his career, though, Rollins is as technically fallible as the leader who plays poorly throughout the session.

He sounds even more uneasy a couple of months later on a recording with Lee Konitz, and there is a story that he tried to flee the studio, having failed to hit his notes on the complex theme statement of George Russell's "Ezz-thetic" (a tune named after one of Miles's favourite boxers, Ezzard Charles). Here, drugs were certainly to blame, but Miles's creative choices during 1951 also suggest an uncertainty as to his most effective direction.

After the demise of the nonet, he can hardly be blamed for wanting to pursue a more commercial line, but his choice of musicians for the first

Prestige recording is significant. None of the white players from the *Birth of the Cool* sessions was retained and pianist John Lewis is the only point of continuity. Miles's choice of Rollins over Konitz was a significant move towards a blacker, hard bop sound, with drummer Roy Haynes providing a hefty but still subtle backbeat, much more linear in approach to the textured music of the nonet. The only audible carry-over was the recruitment of a trombone player, Bennie Green, who fills out the harmonies on three of the four tracks and plays some effective solos.

Green's presence helps steer Miles's composition "Down" in a cooler, more abstract direction, but the basic thrust of the group was conservative. "Blue Room" is a ballad by Miles's favourite Broadway composers Rodgers and Hart, but he fumbles both surviving performances and the issued track is spliced together, a foretaste of the studio techniques that lay behind his great albums of the late 1960s; Miles may also have played piano on one of the versions.

It was a bleak start to a bad year. Miles played very little over the summer but in October had somehow marshalled enough self-possession, physical energy and live playing experience to record his first truly significant session as a bandleader and his first for an LP record. It was released as *Dig,* after one of the original tunes. Unlike Charlie Parker, who could compress a universe of musical wisdom into just a couple of ultra-fast choruses, Miles preferred to let solo ideas evolve, using space and texture rather than sheer technique to get his ideas across. Longer recording durations made that possible. Though he is clearly still not in good physical condition - failing to make notes well within the reach of an amateur player - he solos magnificently and at length on seven substantial tunes.

His playing on "My Old Flame" and "It's Only a Paper Moon", two standard tunes which came towards the end of the session, is delicate and fine and shows something of the debt he owed to singer Frank Sinatra who could invest even a banal lyric with gravitas and real emotion by altering his dynamics and emphasis with infinite subtlety. Miles might almost be singing his lines, so un-idiomatic and un-brasslike is his trumpet tone, but in the years since he began playing professionally he had learned a huge repertoire of non-canonical effects, not one of them encouraged in the rehearsal rooms at Juilliard. He bends and slurs notes, punches and then elides his attacks so that some tones seem almost percussive, while others simply float into hearing and then disappear as mysteriously.

Miles's own disappearance was enough to prompt headlines in the music press, who nonetheless continued to announce his pre-eminence in readers' polls. He was winner of the *Metronome* trumpet category in 1951, 1952 and 1953, when he was ironically at a lower ebb than at any time in his career, apart from his illnesses of the 1970s. For much of the time, he worked out of town and spent some a period back home with his father in St Louis, where in the spring of 1952 he worked with local saxophonist Jimmy Forrest, composer of "Night Train". He'd also struck up a friendship with drummer Philly Joe Jones, another junkie, and the two found some work on the road, though mostly with local musicians.

He did, however, manage to record a short residency at Birdland in May of that year with mellophone and vibraharp player Don Elliott and teenage saxophonist Jackie McLean, a disciple of Bird's who'd featured strongly on the October 5, 1952 session; Parker is said to have been present to give his questionable blessing. At the end of the Birdland residency, Miles recorded half a dozen tracks for a new label, Blue Note, which was to become the pre-eminent jazz imprint of the 1950s and 1960s, though not a long-term association for the trumpeter. He made further recordings for the label in April 1953 and early the following spring. On these he for the most part seems to tread water, revisiting some of his own earlier compositions and otherwise playing compositions and arrangements by associates J. J. Johnson, the pre-eminent bebop trombonist, and saxophonist Jimmy Heath, who though he had switched to the tenor saxophone was known as "Little Bird".

Miles's last documented studio recording with Parker was made for Prestige at the end of January 1953, the occasion where Parker made his own solitary appearance on tenor saxophone. They were briefly heard together again in a live spot with Dizzy Gillespie's group, but Parker's brief, meteoric life was almost over. He died on March 12 1955.

Despite his poll wins, Miles was in danger of being overlooked on a scene where new "stars" are born every minute. Dizzy Gillespie's high-flying style and eccentric demeanour made him a natural draw; Miles had come third to him in the 1949 *Metronome* poll, just behind the brilliant Fats Navarro, who Miles briefly replaced in Tadd Dameron's group. "Fat Girl", as Navarro was cruelly nicknamed, died in July 1950, of tuberculosis exacerbated by heroin abuse; he was just 27. There were other young pretenders knocking at the gates. Thirty-two year old Howard McGhee, who'd also owed his first recording date as leader to Charlie Parker's waywardness, was making fine records for Blue Note, despite succumbing to drugs himself; another Parker employee Red Rodney was overcoming his habit - Miles was briefly admitted to the same Kentucky clinic, but fled - and making an independent career. The brilliant Clifford Brown had played with Miles and Fats Navarro in Philadelphia in 1948 and was establishing a reputation. Ironically, though he kept himself clean of heroin and other drugs, Brown spent the latter half of 1951 laid up after a car crash. Another was to kill him five years later, but by then "Brownie" had gone on to be the most talked-about trumpeter in jazz, putting the still-recovering Miles in eclipse. All the while, on the West Coast, yet another young man with a horn was forging a reputation in Gerry Mulligan's pianoless quartet. Chet Baker's cool approach and papery vocals were matched by chiselled good looks which were still untarnished by narcotics. The "white Miles Davis" made hay while the real Miles Davis was off the scene.

It is hard to imagine what physical and mental anguish Miles underwent as he cleaned his body of drugs, but it is clear that the fanatical discipline which accompanied his detoxification also lent him new musical insights. If there is any truth in the superstition that lives go in seven year cycles, Miles Davis seemed to confirm it. The years between his glorious debut with Charlie Parker and 1954 were dark and troubled and regular employment was still difficult to sustain, but the recording sessions the 28 year old made in 1954 re-established him as a significant innovator and a player of heartbreaking beauty.

His muted solo on "It Never Entered My Mind", another Richard

A studio portrait of Chet Baker and his trumpet. 1954

Rodgers tune and the final item of his Blue Note date of March 6, is a modern classic. It marks a clear declaration of independence from bebop, Miles's playing is spare, unmannered and unshowy in its emotion, and like the other tunes on the date, much of its interest is subtly rhythmic as well as harmonic. Despite the falterings of previous years, Miles confirms his mastery of time and space. This was a quality he learned from pianist Ahmad Jamal, who had been recommended to him by his sister Dorothy. From Jamal's trios he learned how to ease and blur the hierarchy between lead instrument and rhythm section. Miles would further demonstrate that understanding later in the year when he had elements of his group - sometimes the drummer, sometimes the pianist - drop out for certain passages, heightening the tension and drama considerably. This was to be a significant element of the supposedly unprecedented ensemble sound of the late 1960s recordings as well.

There were to be another five studio appearances - all for Prestige - between March and Christmas Eve 1954. All are impressive, but not all are completely satisfying. Along the way, Miles demonstrated his often dormant gift for the blues with "Blue Haze" on March 15, a session which also confirmed a showman's instinct for mood manipulation, by taping the tune with all the studio lights switched off, the kind of trick he was to employ many times over the years to jolt his musicians into new paths of creativity. The first two dates of the year were made with a quartet - the funky Horace Silver on piano, Percy Heath bass and Art Blakey drums - a setting which made Miles's horn the main voice. Back in the studio on April 3, he unaccountably added an alto saxophonist, not Jackie McLean or the ailing Parker, but the almost forgotten Dave Schildkraut, who is competent enough but by no means a convincing soloist.

The first hints of greatness come in the otherwise unsuccessful recording of April 29. Miles recalled trombonist J. J. Johnson and brought in saxophonist Lucky Thompson, often said to be the first player to translate the fast, intense transitions of bebop to the tenor instrument. With no rehearsal time, Miles tried to record some of Thompson's arrangements, but these were not successful and have apparently been lost. Forced to create a "head" arrangement on the spot Miles came up with two spontaneous blues themes, "Walkin'" and "Blue'n'Boogie". The former is an archetypal Miles performance and an essential study point for anyone interested in his art. Though Thompson's fine solo is the dramatic high point of the piece, Miles picks up strong rhythmic clues from replacement drummer Kenny Clarke and delivers seven choruses that swing powerfully without denting the theme's lyricism. As ever in his work, there is an almost anguished undercurrent to the solo. "Blue'n'Boogie" is much faster, but no less effective, and demonstrates how deeply versed Miles was in jazz tradition. In moving forward, he had also reached back into the history of the music.

Were these not such fine performances, they might seem thin return for a day's work in the studio. Two months later to the day, he picked up where he had left off. The June 29 session is important because it introduced a sound which was to be Miles's signature for the rest of his career. Instead of the cup mute, which offered a limited array of effects, Miles opted to play with a metal Harmon mute, a familiar enough device whose central plunger allowed a trumpeter to vary his sound considerably. Idiosyncratic as ever, Miles opted to remove the plunger, yielding a tone which was either mournful and intimate or sharp depending on the pitch and attack of the note.

Miles recalled Sonny Rollins for the date and the saxophonist brought in two themes, "Airegin" ("Nigeria" backwards) and "Oleo", which became repertory staples for jazz groups. Based, like so many bebop themes, on the chords of "I Got Rhythm", "Oleo" showcased Miles's new sound in a brilliantly witty, totally unexpected performance which, along with "Now's The Time" for Parker, and "Walkin'", is a benchmark in his recorded career.

Recording was increasingly essential for a jazz musican. With the advent of the LP, discs were major statements. The longer durations allowed soloists of Miles's stamp to develop ideas more fully. He had much to thank Weinstock for, as the final recording session of 1954, taped on Christmas Eve with vibraphonist Milt Jackson, Percy Heath and Kenny Clarke of Prestige signings the Modern Jazz Quartet, succeeded despite rather than because of the personalities involved. Also present was the eccentric Thelonious Monk, to whom Miles owed an admiring debt but who he regarded as a problematic accompanist. The trumpet solos on "The Man I Love" and Jackson's "Bags' Groove" are not supported by piano, apparently at Miles's insistence. Elsewhere on the record Monk seems detached from what the other musicians are playing.

However grateful he must have been to Weinstock for signing him at a low ebb in his fortunes, Miles was conscious that his art required a significantly higher level of investment. Now that he had successfully battled his drug demons - though there were other personal problems on the horizon - he could look forward.

Post-Bird

Charlie Parker died on March 12 1955, succumbing to a heart attack in the New York apartment of the Baroness Pannonica de Koenigswarter, who later became Thelonious Monk's patron. Famously the doctor who attended Bird thought he was dealing with a man around 60 years of age. Parker was 34.

It's a tiny irony of musical history that Miles Davis, who learned so much and so ambiguously from Parker should have been in prison when he passed away. Irene had pursued him for maintenance - there were now three children from the relationship - and was eventually forced to invoke the law. It's a sign that all was still not well with Miles. The first six months of 1955 saw another period of inactivity, but typically the trumpeter managed to snatch something from the jaws of defeat. He made three separate and qualitatively different recording sessions during the summer. In June, he experimented with another quartet format, again with Philly Joe Jones, but this time using pianist Red Garland and the turbulent Oscar Pettiford on bass. Even staunch fans have found it difficult to enjoy these half dozen cuts. Miles's intonation is faulty, he hits wrong notes throughout and never sounds completely in tune with Garland.

Exactly a month later, he was reunited with another volcanic personality, Charles Mingus, recording four of the bassist's arrangements for his Debut label. Miles's playing is transformed, clear and expressive on a vintage version of "Nature Boy". But he was still looking for a stable group of his own and Mingus presumably wasn't interested or able to commit to someone else's project. There was another fine recording in August with Jackie Mclean and Milt Jackson, with Ray Bryant, Percy Heath and Art Taylor completing the rhythm section, but Miles was still minded to

Miles' producer George Avakian also worked with Louis Armstrong and Dave Brubeck

develop the quartet he'd aired so unsatisfactorily in June, except that the quartet was destined to become his first important quintet.

Not for the first time, Miles experimented with youth, hiring the 20 year old Paul Chambers. In his short life, the Pittsburgh-born bassist transformed the instrument's role in small-group jazz, bringing a full, well-rounded tone and, more important, the subtle sense of time that Miles demanded. Even more important though, was his eventual choice of saxophone player. Miles had been keen to re-hire his junkie friend Sonny Rollins on a more permanent basis, but he was persuaded by Philly Joe Jones to listen instead to a young man originally from North Carolina, but working out of the drummer's home town of Philadelphia. His name was John Coltrane.

It's never been difficult to mythologise the differences of temperament and musical personality of Miles Davis and John Coltrane. Where Miles was terse, taut, combative, "the Prince of Darkness", Coltrane seemed a gentler and more reflective man, bent on a spiritual quest. The most famous - probably overquoted - anecdote about them relates to the moment when Miles lost patience at one of Trane's endless, introspective solos. "Why do you play so many notes?", "I don't know how to stop", "Just take the horn out of your mouth." Not for nothing was Coltrane born in a small town called Hamlet. At times, he seems all hesitation and self-doubt, while Miles is always prepared to wait for the psychological moment and deliver a phrase so right for the context that it might almost have been pre-planned.

In reality, Coltrane's calm was hard-won. He, too, battled with drug and alcohol addiction and even in later years dabbled with hallucinogens. Some of the immensely long, harmonically extreme solos he created with his own legendary quartet were played on LSD. When he first met Miles, though, he was a virtual unknown and it is characteristic of the trumpeter's perspicacity that he recognised the talent behind the few slightly awkward and diffident solos Coltrane had so far committed to record. Together they were to create an extraordinary body of music and, in March and April 1959, would collaborate on what many still regard as the finest jazz album ever made.

In the summer of 1955, though, Miles was just climbing out of the doldrums. The key moment career-wise that summer was a triumphant appearance at the Newport Jazz Festival, established the year before but already a prestigious showcase for new and established jazz talent. As well as winning him a new and relatively well-off (i.e. white) audience, it brought him back to the attention of producer George Avakian of Columbia Records, who Miles had already approached on a couple of occasions, and in a single appearance propelled him towards another poll win in *Down Beat*, who also featured Miles in the magazine's legendary "Blindfold Test".

Bankable once again, he began to chafe against the restrictions imposed by his Prestige contract. Weinstock could not or would not pay for rehearsal time, which meant that recordings for the label were usually spontaneous and shambolic, relying on loose "head" arrangements and a hurriedly agreed chord structure rather than the detailed charts of the *Birth of the Cool* sessions. Miles was enough of a Juilliard formalist to resent a way of recording that no classical musician would have tolerated for a moment; to him, jazz was art, not just entertainment music, and required a level of investment that Prestige simply could not deliver. Ironically, his working practices were such that, even in a more relaxed environment, with no need to keep an eye on the clock and with plenty of time for rehearsal, Miles continued to work spontaneously, often working from rapidly sketched ideas (perhaps a legacy of his time with Parker) and usually preferring a single "take" of each tune or theme.

Though the new quintet is firmly associated with his old label, thanks to an extraordinary concentration of studio work in 1956 and the eventual release of four superb albums, its first formal recording was for Columbia. This was the result of careful diplomacy, involving Weinstock, Avakian and Miles's manager Harold Lovett. The agreement was that he should honour his contract to Prestige (hence four records from just two sessions) but that he could record for Columbia in the meantime.

The new group had been heard on radio in October, from a New York City club, shortly before that first tentative Columbia date, but its first substantial studio work was done on November 17, for an album called, significantly, *The New Miles Davis Quintet*. There are signs that the trumpeter and saxophonist have not yet completely gelled. Miles generally avoids ensemble intros, preferring to let one horn or the other state the theme. The exception is "Stablemates", a composition by saxophonist

Miles Davis at a performance in 1955

Benny Golson, and the sound is unattractively ragged. Coltrane drops out altogether on "There Is No Greater Love", which is arguably Miles's best solo of the set. He also includes "Miles's Theme", yet another variant on the "I Got Rhythm" chords which, as "The Theme", was to be a staple of his live act for years, often used to close a set or fill in time before a radio commercial break.

Coltrane has yet to develop the iron-hard intonation of later years and some of his playing is characterless. Miles, by contrast, sounds articulate and very strong, using his mute to great effect and producing ever subtler dynamics in his solos. His phrasing is taut and limber, and often seems to float free of the rhythm section, who play with unusual freedom for the period. Here can be heard once again the influence of Ahmad Jamal, who remained a firm favourite.

Between October 1955 and October 26 1956, Miles was in the studio nine times, including two further sessions for Columbia, eventually released as *Round About Midnight*. He also appeared as soloist with composer and musicologist Gunther Schuller's Brass Ensemble of the Jazz and Classical Music Society, looks back to the *Birth of the Cool* sessions but also forward to Miles's historic orchestral recordings with Gil Evans. (It is significant for another reason as well.) The important work, though, was reserved for the four further albums from 1956 released as *Relaxin'*, *Workin'*, *Cookin'* and *Steamin'* (The earlier *Walkin'* is unrelated, product of the April 1954 date with J. J. Johnson, Dave Schildkraut and Lucky Thompson.) Cleverly, Prestige released the records over a five year period, so that even when Miles was an established Columbia artist he was still associated with his old label.

They are uneven in inspiration, but at their greatest they bespeak an extraordinary sense of spontaneity, a brilliant assemblage of players in creative flux; a similar impression to those experimental bebop sessions with Parker, except that the advent of the LP era allowed for longer and more substantial performance than on careful attention to the sequencing of tracks. The strongest audible contrast is between Miles - spare, introverted, guileful - and the bristling, leonine Coltrane, still at a somewhat chaotic stage in his development. Equally telling, though, are the members of the rhythm section, who contrived to create a different context behind each soloist even as they sustain the logical flow of the themes. The sound thickens and intensifies behind Coltrane, floods with air and light behind Red Garland as if a window has been thrown open, toys with playful ambiguity behind Miles.

Recorded at a handful of marathon sessions, each record has its special rewards: a slow, pierced "My Funny Valentine" on *Cookin'*, and a truly haunted version of "It Never Entered My Mind" on *Workin'*, the supple swing of "I Could Write A Book" and revitalised bebop of "Woody'n'You" on *Relaxin';* the same chemistry works brilliantly on *Steamin'*, where the medium-paced "Surrey With The Fringe On Top" is followed by the bebop classic "Salt Peanuts". As the titles suggest, Miles showed a shrewd understanding that the public would warm more quickly to arrangements of familiar Broadway songs than to original melodies or themeless "heads". He also understood the virtues of an instantly recognisable instrumental "voice". Though quickly imitated by others, his use of the Harmon mute gave his playing a personality as distinctive as Frank Sinatra's, intimate, wry, elegiac rather than conventionally bluesy, suffused with anger.

Coltrane's style also reflected his personality and hinted at what was going on behind the scenes. Egged on by Philly Joe, the saxophonist was slipping deeper into his drug habit, often exacerbated by excessive drinking. On more than one occasion, Miles was seen to abuse a near-comatose Trane verbally and physically, and in March 1957, patience finally exhausted, he fired the saxophonist, and sent Philly Joe packing after him. A prodigious year in the studio, ending with a successful return to Europe for Miles, had taken its toll. Exhausted, distressed about parting with a close friend, albeit temporarily, and perhaps aware he had flooded the market with new records, he even announced his intention to retire. Another parallel to Sinatra?

Nontheless, 1956 established Miles Davis as a formidable player on the jazz scene. He had all but perfected his approach to small group playing, demonstrating a mastery that was more instinctive than intellectual, certainly not slave to any harmonic or compositional system. And he had not only consolidated a new instrumental voice, but in the session of October 20 for Gunther Schuller, pioneered a new jazz instrument, also immediately and widely imitated. All that remained was the return into his career of an inspirational collaborator.

Svengali

Gil Evans is an anagram of Svengali, a chance bit of wordplay later seized on for an album title. In reality, nothing could be further from the truth. Evans' personality was as austere and reserved as his working methods were shambolic, but he brought an equal ease in jazz and classical music, and with Miles's Prestige contract agreeably concluded and his move to Columbia confirmed, Evans offered a chance to revive and develop an idiom that had stalled with the disintegration of the nonet.

There was a seven year gap in their association, but while Miles had gone through agonies of addiction and self-doubt, Evans had continued on his quiet, ascetic path, absorbing vast amounts of music and music history. They were an unlikely pairing, though no more unlikely than Duke Ellington and Billy Strayhorn, and the music they made together amply deserves the comparison. Miles Davis and Gil Evans *heard* music in a similar way. The association continued over an eleven year period and intermittently beyond, though the classics fall into a six year span during which Miles also recorded some of his finest small group work, including his most celebrated album *Kind of Blue*, and it is clear that Evans's mastery of orchestral forms also had a profound influence on Miles's small combo work.

It's important that that mastery was largely self-acquired. Evans' sense of how an orchestra functioned was coloured by his listening experience in African and South American music, very different to the classical conventions taught at a music school like Juilliard. Since this was the very training Miles had turned his back on, Evans' unorthodox approach was bound to appeal. Using middle- to low-toned instruments like bass trombone, tenor saxophones, bass clarinet and tuba as well as string bass and drums (but no piano, interestingly, but for a few measures on "Springsville") Evans created a swirling, harmonically rich and rhythmically subtle environment for his soloist. Despite the inclusion of a five-strong trumpet section, three flutes and an alto saxophone, the overall sound was pitched at a level much more conducive to Miles's middle-register soloing and plangency of tone than a conventional jazz orchestra.

Miles responded by changing his instrument of choice. Though he never repeated the experiment, scores of trumpeters immediately imitated him, and do to this day. He had dabbled with the flugelhorn the previous October with Gunther Schuller's Brass Ensemble, but *Miles Ahead* brought an unfashionable horn, normally only heard in brass bands, to the forefront of an innovatively structured jazz suite. Though singles were released from the album, it was its seamless organisation as well as Miles's haunting solo voice that made it unique. The flugelhorn has a slightly fuller, "fatter" sound that trumpet and a much less incisive attack, making it ideal for this music. One reviewer of the album talked about Evans moving "out of the proper realm of jazz", by which he presumably not only meant its continuous, suite-like structure, but also the inclusion of a radically reworked classical composition, Leo Delibes' "The Maids of Cadiz".

Miles was aware that in taking a new direction (and that phrase was to become a marketing device later) he might be seem to be turning his back on hard bop and small group work. He had disbanded his quintet to concentrate on *Miles Ahead*, which was recorded in four marathon sessions in May. He recorded nothing else that spring, but seemed to throw himself into what was to be another lifetime endeavour: the creation of the complex, iconic personality that was "Miles Davis".

As well as winning trumpet polls (and *Miles Ahead* put him squarely back on top, even if he'd briefly set aside his main horn), Miles was beginning to appear in mainstream magazines, and in roles that as often as not did not require a musical instrument at all: Miles the fashionplate, Miles the boxer, horserider, driver of fast cars. At the same time, he cultivated a combative demeanour (sometimes physically so) with the press and recalcitrant musicians, shrugging off praise or awards,

Miles seen here with Gil Evans in a studio recording session

answering questions with questions, lapsing into silence if he didn't like the turn the conversation was taking. (It was a lesson taken to heart by Prince, the precocious young R&B star Miles befriended in the 1980s.) The factor that completed the image was Miles's speaking voice, formerly crisp and well-educated - compare his early stage announcement with Charlie Parker's high-pitched waffle - but now reduced to a throaty growl by nodes on the vocal chords. After the completion of *Miles Ahead*, he underwent surgery to remove the polyps and was instructed to rest his voice for a period thereafter. Whether this also involved laying off trumpet playing isn't clear, but Miles was instructed to rest his vocal cords for a time. Famously, he defied doctor's orders by shouting at a music business figure (some versions say it was his agent), permanently damaging his voice. For the rest of his life, he spoke in an eerie whisper. On his last concert tours, he even held up name cards to introduce his bands rather than calling out their names.

The trumpet voice was unimpaired. His soloing on *Miles Ahead* is rich and deeply affecting. The slightly unfamiliar timbre renders it unique among his albums, but, like Charlie Parker playing tenor saxophone, still immediately recognisable. His playing on "The Maids of Cadiz", "Blues for Pablo" and the Ahmad Jamal composition "New Rhumba" is of the highest order.

Miles played very little for the rest of the year, though one session - recorded on the fly in Paris - was to have a significant impact on his later thinking as will be seen later. Whether he was still unsure about his creative direction or whether he had intuited that a Garbo-like demeanour was more effective commercially than the flurry of activity that had led to *Workin', Cookin', Relaxin'* and *Steamin'* is a further matter of surmise.

What is absolutely clear is his dependence on Gil Evans. They worked together again in July 19 on a brilliant jazz realisation of George Gershwin's operatic musical *Porgy and Bess*. In terms of combining Evans's unorthodox classical interests and Miles's equally idiosyncratic but also deeply traditional jazz approach there could be no more inspirational source material. It is immediately clear from the record that in his relationship with Evans the centre of gravity had shifted somewhat. This is emphatically Miles Davis's record and closer to the kind of one-take spontaneity that he had favoured before and would ever after. The orchestral playing is far from pristine, but whereas on *Miles Ahead* it served as a *ripieno* to the *concertante* playing of the soloist, here it serves as little more than an accompaniment to solo playing of genuine grandeur and scarifying power. Ian Carr has shrewdly likened the effect to the call-and-response of preacher and congregation in the Sanctified church.

"Prayer" is ecstatic and intense, a virtuoso trumpet performance that looks forward to the one-chord improvisations of the soon to be recalled John Coltrane. Again, though, Miles takes the opposite musical tack to his erstwhile saxophonist; where Coltrane would have plunged deep into the harmonic mysteries of the theme, Miles radically simplifies them, paring down his material to a biblical starkness. On "It Ain't Necessarily So" he scarcely moves outside the bounds of the song, but opens up dramas within it that even the composer could only have guessed at. On "Summertime", his muted solo is again a meditation on the melody rather than an improvisation on its chords; indeed, one long passage marks a further exploration of what can be done over just one chord, with virtually no harmonic movement.

If *Miles Ahead* is virtually uncategorisable, *Porgy and Bess* is unmistakably a jazz album. Back on his familiar horn, Miles deploys all the techniques at his disposal, long, swooping tones, tense, half-valved sounds, slurs and growls, and a use of space and syncopation that again recalls Louis Armstrong. Every note is made to count, and the stereo sound - *Porgy and Bess* was Miles's first stereophonic release - gives the music extra presence. Miles was still not in the best physical shape and seemed exhausted by the sessions. Nevertheless, they represent a pinnacle in his career to date.

Though he had reconvened his small group in the spring of 1958, he was no longer in a hurry to record, experimenting with the sound of an

Miles lost no opportunity to flirt, here he plays for Jeanne Moreau

53

augmented line-up. For the moment, though, his attention was divided between combo jazz and a fruitfully eclectic collaboration with Evans. They were back in the studio again in November 1959 to record an album which, along with *Kind of Blue*, John Coltrane's *A Love Supreme* and a Billie Holiday anthology can be found even in record collections that include no other jazz records.

Much has been said, misleadingly, about what Jelly Roll Morton described as the "Spanish tinge" in jazz. *Sketches of Spain* is a wonderful creation by any standard. Its confident appropriation of classical repertoire, in the opening version of Rodrigo's *Concierto de Aranjuez* and a selection from Manuel de Falla's ballet *El amor brujo,* made it an early version of that contemporary chimera, the "crossover hit". It also reflected Gil Evans's fascination with flamenco: "Saeta" and "Solea". Heard with the hindsight of forty five years, it's a less radical project than it would have appeared at the time. There is a deliberate openness in the orchestration, which means that individual players appear as themselves rather than as cogs in an ensemble. Even when playing Evans's written parts, they sound as if they might be improvising. The harmonic and rhythmic basis of the music is unusual by the standards of the time, using scales rather than chords and creating an illusion of movement where actually there is only texture. The other aspect of the album that was radical was that it was very largely a production artefact, edited down from many hours of studio tapes by a brilliantly gifted producer/engineer who was to play a vitally important role in Miles's subsequent career. Teo Macero fulfilled a different role, but he was to become a collaborator every bit as important as Gil Evans.

Again, much as they did on *Porgy and Bess,* Miles and Evans used the trajectory of a two-sided LP to dramatise a shift in musical thinking from the European-classical (the Rodrigo and De Falla) to the African-American. One wonders how many fans who cherished the album before its CD reissue turned to the second side where Miles presents himself less as an instrumentalist than as an impassioned singer of *cante jondo*, the "deep song" that is Spain's equivalent of the blues, and both musically and expressively a near relative. His solos on "Saeta" and "Solea" hints at a recognition that would also fuel Miles's later years: that jazz is not so much a noun as a verb, a way of playing music rather than a body of existing material. These themes were as alien to the jazz audience in 1959 as Scritti Politi and Michael Jackson songs would be in the 1980s.

Sketches of Spain was the climax of Miles's association with Gil Evans. The two had worked together earlier in the spring of 1959 on a television special that brought their music to a wider audience (though not the promised network millions) and would collaborate once more in 1962 on a programme of Antonio Carlos Jobim material which, despite both musicians' reluctance, was released by Columbia as *Quiet Nights*, one of the few genuinely disappointing releases in the whole Miles Davis canon.

Its innovations brought into focus a new strand of the trumpeter's musical thinking, an approach to composition and playing which he happened upon almost accidentally in Paris back in December 1957 when Miles agreed to record soundtrack music for the Louis Malle thriller *L'Ascenseur pour l'echafaud* (in English, *Lift for the Scaffold*). Working with French musicians who were competent but relatively unsophisticated, Miles could not have played any of his own recent compositions, so the music was freely improvised on the basis of an agreed tempo and a notional tonality. In a single after-midnight session he recorded ten impressionistic fragments that perfectly underline the film's existentialist mood, but which also suggested to him a new way out of the labyrinth of bebop harmony. Miles's playing alternates between limpid beauty and a fierce abstraction that is the first shadowing of the dark, dangerous work he was to play in the late 1960s and 1970s. Interestingly, the project that added fresh impetus to that new style was another film, a documentary about heavyweight boxing champion Jack Johnson and his battle against white racism.

You're Under Arrest

Though he grew up in a respectable, middle-class neighbourhood (or possibly for that very reason) Miles Davis was no stranger to racial prejudice. He would, at very least, have been aware of a shocking and all too recent history of racial violence in St Louis. He experienced it in milder form at Juilliard, where black students were still in a small minority. It reared again at the peak of his success.

In the summer of 1959, a matter of weeks after recording his masterpiece *Kind of Blue*, Miles was playing at Birdland with his sextet. Between sets, he escorted a white woman friend out onto Broadway and flagged a cab for her. He was observed by two policemen who told him to move on. Though Miles explained he was working in the club, one of the officers threatened him with arrest. Miles remonstrated and while the two were arguing, the second policeman struck him from behind with a billy club, beating him several more times as he lay on the ground, where like Rodney King more than thirty years later he was presumably "resisting arrest".

To compound the brutal absurdity of the situation, Miles was charged with assault and stripped of his cabaret card. Fortunately, it was hard to walk more than a block on Broadway in 1959 without encountering a press photographer with a SpeedGraphic camera. Pictures of jazz's new star spattered with blood went round the world. Conscious of the bad publicity, and certainly aware that Miles's manager Harold Lovett was consulting lawyers, a judge threw out the case.

It all added to the trumpeter's fatal glamour. When later he pointed out, in that eerie whisper, that the guilty cop had himself been killed, it was hard not to take away the impression that Miles might have been involved; at least, that is what he wanted you to think. The gangsters who fired shots at him in the autumn of 1969, wounding Miles in the leg but missing his girlfriend Marguerite Eskridge, were also apparently killed. Miles took pains to point out that being targeted by fellow-outsiders was far less traumatic than being beaten by the cops. As if to underline the parallel with ten years before, Miles and Marguerite were ticketed for marijuana possession.

Less than a year later, he was arrested for driving an unregistered and unlicensed vehicle and for possession of a set of brass knuckles. Central Manhattan wasn't and isn't Alabama, but the sight of an exotically dressed black man in a red Ferrari still seemed to inspire unreasoning resentment.

Miles Davis rarely made overtly political comments. Carr's biography has no index entry for "politics" under his name. From time to time, he made it clear that he supported decriminalisation of drug use and he spoke up strongly against racial prejudice, but unlike many of his artistic peers - John Coltrane, Charles Mingus, Max Roach - he made few explicit attempts to give his music a polemical cast. His soundtrack music for William Clayton's documentary film on boxer Jack Johnson is undeniably passionate and sincere, but like the music for *L'ascenseur pour l'echafaud,* it is more significant for its experimentalism than for its programmatic content. Talking to a French interviewer in the 1980s, he admitted that he didn't feel it was his place to comment on the *apartheid* system in South Africa, beyond the small gesture of solidarity implicit in calling two of his later albums *Tutu* (after the charismatic Bishop of Cape Town) and *Amandla.* Though he shared his father's intense pride in an African-American heritage and despised those who (like his mother, perhaps) craved acceptance in white society, Miles rarely went out of his way to declare his *negritude,* either overtly or exclusively. The term "radical chic" was coined by Tom Wolfe to describe conductor Leonard Bernstein's extraordinary, uncomfortable lionisation of the Black Panthers; Miles steered away from any public association. His radicalism was of an entirely different stamp, his chic entirely personal. (He did, however, host a party for Robert Kennedy, during his election campaign for a New York senate seat; with perverse inevitability, Leonard Bernstein was one of the guests.) The only

Caught on stage in a photo essay for Time Magazine. 1958

one of his records which has separatist overtones is the controversial *On The Corner*, on whose cover Miles seems to align himself with a hip, black constituency.

Something of that personality and allegiance was already in place a decade earlier. By the close of the 1950s, Miles Davis was one of the most

visible black men in America, and one of the most visible black Americans on a world stage, even more passionately admired in Europe than at home. At a time when many jazz artists, bruised by prejudice, migrated to France and Scandinavia, attracted by their tolerant and enthusiastic audiences, Miles remained at home, for all his ambivalence an American artist to his core. He was handsome, increasingly rich, married to the beautiful Frances (a dancer whom he'd met in California), beguilingly dangerous and enigmatic. The "Prince of Darkness" tag, borrowed from a composition by saxophonist Wayne Shorter, was lying in wait for him. For the moment, he looked, acted and played like a flawed angel, Lucifer, Star of the Morning.

In the autumn of 1957, Miles had set about reconvening his small group. He still seemed content to work intermittently, but having a regular outlet for his music was both a creative and commercial necessity.

Unfortunately, during the group's hiatus his original sidemen had found work elsewhere, leaving Miles to experiment with a new rhythm section (pianist Tommy Flanagan, drummer Art Taylor) and a new saxophonist. He briefly hired the Belgian exile Bobby Jaspar, who sounded like a pale imitation of the great Lester Young, but quickly replaced him with alto saxophonist Julian 'Cannonball' Adderley, a larger-than-life figure with an intense, blues-drenched tone. Almost more important, though, Adderley was free of drugs. A gentle giant, he became the new group's "straw boss", handling band fees and other arrangements. Miles's respect and affection for him can be measured by his willingness to guest on Adderley's own Blue Note record *Somethin' Else*, recorded in March 1958, a full month before Miles's own first recording as leader for nearly a year; his studio diary for 1957 was limited to the *Miles Ahead* sessions and the deceptively casual *L'ascenseur pour l'echafaud*.

His generosity to Adderley was unfeigned, but Miles had also been biding his time, hoping to lure back Red Garland and Philly Joe Jones; a risky commitment, since both, like bassist Paul Chambers, were still serious heroin users. The other sought-after recruit had managed to kick his habit. John Coltrane, the man Miles had punched and abused in sheer frustration, had spent much of 1957 working with pianist Thelonious Monk, building on his formidable harmonic understanding, and working on his health. He returned to Miles's employ sober, thoughtful, marked by a spirituality that was by no means new but which had been eclipsed by narcotics, and possessed of an ironclad technique which gave the sextet a third distinctive solo voice.

Such was the power of the three solo horns that they dominate *Milestones*, the album the sextet cut on April 2 and 3 1958. As a sop to the pianist, Miles allowed him to play one trio track with just bass and drums and clearly Garland feels enormous respect for Miles's musicianship since he copies the trumpeter's November 1945 "Now's The Time" solo more or less note for note during his feature on "Straight, No Chaser". For the rest, though, Garland is barely in evidence, except as an accompanist. He was so disenchanted by his position that he apparently walked out of the studio on the second day. The aural evidence is on the slow blues "Sid's Ahead", where the horns state the theme without piano chords. Miles's solo has no chordal accompaniment, while those by Coltrane and Adderley do. The reason? Miles himself took over piano duties and in doing so demonstrates his growing harmonic mastery. It's a stark and moving performance, based on Miles's own early blues "Weirdo", but infused with such feeling that Coltrane's and Adderley's following statements seem by comparison sententious or trivial respectively.

Two other factors stand out on *Milestones*. One is that Miles plays open horn throughout, with no use of his Harmon mute. The other is a brief reappearance of the flugelhorn on the title track which is another virtuosically simple idea enhanced by subtle shifts of metre in the rhythm section. Here and throughout the album Miles appears to be exploring territory he had first visited on *L'ascenseur pour l'echafaud*. In particular, he builds complex solo ideas out of simple scales rather than a chord structure, a device that makes the music sound ageless and grand, primal rather than primitive, the musical equivalent of a Shona sculpture or Mayan head.

Carr describes *Milestones* as "transitional". That's an undeniable description, but also an empty one, since scarcely a single session recorded by Miles between 1945 and 1991 sounds like a comfortable consolidation. The "curse" of change was upon him from the beginning, though some aspects of it were enforced by circumstance rather than choice. In Coltrane, he had a sideman who was deeply involved in his own explorations, piling one chord on another, playing counter to the harmony, or half-steps away from it, sometimes seeming to worry at one idea over many measures irrespective of the chords or melody. But at least the Coltrane of 1958 was reliable. Not so Garland, Chambers and Jones. All three were still addicts but also, as rhythm section players, much in demand by other group leaders. Miles's dream of a stable group seemed compromised from the moment he fulfilled it. In the later spring of 1958, he had to replace his old friend Jones with the more punctilious Jimmy Cobb, and Garland with a quiet, 29 year old white man from Plainfield' New Jersey.

Bill Evans was on the brink of becoming a star in his own right when Miles recruited him. Relative to his influence, his tenure with the sextet was ironically short, but in the months they were together he brought Miles a mixture of lyrical beauty and adamantine control and precision. Though Evans's later life was blighted by drugs and alcohol, he was a model of artistic probity, seemingly egoless. Like his namesake Gil, he was aware of a vast range of music outside jazz, notably Debussy and Ravel, and thus brought a very different sensibility to the ensemble. Where Garland was blues-based and funky, Evans was capable of playing supportive but independent piano lines, delivered with great delicacy of touch. Ironically, he made his greatest and best-loved contribution to Miles Davis's music *after* he had officially left the group.

In the summer of 1958, Miles was preparing to record *Porgy and Bess* with another Evans, but the new pianist can be heard on a brief live session from the Cafe Bohemia, on the tentative May 26 studio date that also saw the introduction of Jimmy Cobb and yielded a classic version of the film theme "On Green Dolphin Street", and as a session player along with Miles, Coltrane and Chambers on a New York recording by French composer/arranger Michel Legrand. Not until the 1980s when Miles began to appear as a guest star on pop albums did he again work on any other leader's project. The first substantial evidence for Evans' contribution to the group comes on a live recording of the sextet made at the Plaza Hotel and subsequently released as *Jazz at the Plaza*. The group sound has evolved yet again into something harmonically ambiguous, floating and enigmatic, with Miles's own approach veering between hostility and an eggshell-stepping delicacy. Evans's ability to play in asymmetrical metres while retaining the basic pulse of a piece is extraordinary, as is his gift for suggesting a tonality while taking his own solo ideas very far from it. It made him the ideal group player, at least in a group as flagrantly original and idiosyncratic as the Miles Davis Sextet.

It also meant he was a loss Miles could not easily sustain. The usually amenable Red Garland was on hand to substitute when Evans left in November 1958, but it wasn't until the following February that Miles permanently replaced him. It is just as well that young Wynton Kelly had little of Garland's fragility of ego, because when the 27 year old turned up on March 2 1959 for what would become Miles's most celebrated recording, he discovered that his employer had also recalled Bill Evans. In the event, both pianists played on the record and the contrast between them - Evans's sombre writing and playing on "Blue in Green", Kelly's almost euphoric blues phrasing on "Freddie Freeloader" - is one of the things that makes the record great.

Evans also wrote the liner notes for the original release, on which he explains that none of the music had been rehearsed before coming into the studio. In reality, Miles had worked and reworked some of these ideas quite thoroughly before. With his gradual abandonment of conventionally harmonic writing and move towards a "scalar" or "modal" approach influenced by the ideas of George Russell, he had continued to build on the loose, improvisational method used for *L'ascenseur pour l'echafaud*. It's an approach that might seem free-form to the point of casualness, but which requires iron discipline and sophisticated harmonic understanding to pull off at the level evinced by *Kind of Blue*.

Again, Miles makes a virtue of apparent simplicity. There are no fast themes on the album, no show-piece standards tunes; everything is quiet, slow to mid-tempo, and thoughtful. One does not remember Miles solos from the record in the way one remembers them from *Milestones* or from the orchestral albumes with Gil Evans. There are fine contrasting solos from all concerned, and some brilliantly varied accompaniment from Evans, who sounds like a different piano player behind Miles or Adderley than when he underplays the brooding Coltrane, but the essence of *Kind of Blue* is its ensemble sound, the work of an artist who has rationalised his palette to explore a limited range of tonalities. It isn't exactly Miles's "Blue Period", more a Whistler-like nocturne in indigos, greys and smoky browns.

The theme of "Freddie Freeloader", a B flat blues, is radically stripped down, its dramatic release all coming from a soft, descending two-note motif. The opening "So What", probably the best-known piece on the album, works in exactly the same way, a call-and-response between the bass and the three horns, who reply "so what?" in exquisite harmony. The track that opened side two, "All Blues", is based on a very similar idea, a repeated three-note figure that had by this time in his career become something of a Miles *leitmotif*; it also forms the basis of "Milestones" (aka "Miles").

"All Blues" and the lean, evanescent "Flamenco Sketches" (a sign that he was working towards the *Sketches of Spain* sessions in November) were taped by Miles and the group at a second, April 22 recording. The bulk of the album had been got down more than a month earlier, by a group that was already fragmenting. Evans proved to be a vital contributor at both sessions, with Kelly kept to the sidelines for now, but it was becoming clear that Coltrane and Adderley, both of whom were still enjoying indifferent health, albeit for different reasons, were also considering their futures outside the Davis group. For the moment, though, it was the most prominent place to be in modern jazz.

A "masterpiece" is a concept born of hindsight. No one present at the March 2 and April 22 1959 sessions had any idea that *Kind of Blue* would become an iconic bestseller, treasured by succeeding generations of jazz fans. "So What" still floats out of the speakers in wine bars and restaurants, familiar even to non-jazz audiences in a way that only Billie Holiday has matched. The rest of the album, as is the fate of iconic records, is probably less well known and less thoroughly examined, but it underlines how brilliantly Miles Davis was able to create and sustain a single mood, to build it out of radically simplified materials, and to bend musicians of such different styles and temperaments to his will. Over-familiar it may have become, its exploratory urge neutralised by generations of imitators, it nonetheless remains one of the half-dozen truly great jazz records.

John Coltrane

Even if Miles Davis had followed through on his occasional threats and retired from active playing at the end of 1959, the appearance of *Kind of Blue* and *Sketches of Spain* would have guaranteed his immortality. As it was, he would continue playing - ever more controversially - for another 32 years.

So What

In December 1960, Miles married Frances Taylor, the *West Side Story* dancer who had inspired the beautiful "Fran-Dance". Their relationship had already lasted for some time, overlapping with the Juliette Greco affair and covering the period of his addiction, but had been conducted intermittently and at a distance. As a touring musician - and as a junkie - Miles didn't make for a reliable partner. However, when she moved from the West Coast to New York, Frances became a regular companion and, like Irene before her, a significant influence. At a time when his health was again faltering after a diagnosis of sickle-cell anaemia, Frances brought a measure of stability to Miles's life, creating a family environment in the converted West 77th Street apartment which housed them and the four children they shared from his time with Irene and from a previous relationship of Frances's. Arguably more important, she opened up for him a whole spectrum of new aesthetic experiences, introducing him to the complex rhythms of non-Western dance when the Ballet Africaine toured the US and teaching him a lot about physical deportment. "Fran-Dance" was a clever little homage, based as it was on the dance tune "Put Your Little Foot Right Out". Unfortunately, Miles's respect only went so far. He made it clear to Frances that marriage meant the end of her public performing career.

Throughout his life, beginning with his mother and sister and extending to the wives and girfriends he routinely refers to as "bitches" in his autobiography, he remained ambivalent about women, with a deep Oedipal unease. He also had strong albeit rarely acknowledged homoerotic feelings, though unlike his brother Vernon, he was bisexual rather than openly gay. His obsessive pursuit of Charlie Parker in 1944 and 1945 was musical hero-worship, but there is a discernible hint of romantic affection in his relationship with John Coltrane, and in his evident fondness in later years for young band members and for other young musicians like Prince.

In 1960 Miles had some of the fatal glamour of a rebellious movie star. He attracted a larger than usual female audience to his club engagements and to concerts like his Newport Festival appearance in July 1958. Miles was easily the most prominent jazz instrumentalist of his day, gradually supplanting the now 60 year old Louis Armstrong as the leading trumpeter in the world and offering an abrasive and more contemporary alternative to "Satchmo"'s avuncular stage persona. The non-music media were fascinated by Miles Davis - his clothes and lifestyle, his frequent flashes of temperament - and created a lasting mythology out of his stage demeanour. Even people who had never seen or heard Miles in a club or on a record knew that he rarely acknowledged applause and played trumpet with his back to the audience, a gesture of contempt to middle-class whites or a sign of his intense concentration on the group, depending on your point of view. His public pronouncements were mostly terse, often studiedly dismissive, and rarely analytical. The only exceptions were the trenchant comments he offered on other musicians' records in his "Blindfold Tests" for *Down Beat* and similar interviews.

At 33, Miles was subject to an extraordinary level of personal scrutiny. It is ironic that his music should have undergone a similar intensity of examination after his death. For much of his lifetime, Miles's records were reviewed as if they were style statements, new phases in a personal mythology. This may be true, but only very partially. Throughout his life, Miles was one hundred percent committed to a musical evolution. The vagaries of the music industry meant that only a fraction of what he recorded was ever issued, not necessarily in a form he approved (the final Gil Evans collaboration *Quiet Night* wasn't approved by either man) and not always in logical order. Not until the 1980s, when Miles Davis concerts were bootlegged on amateur equipment virtually every time he appeared, was there any systematic documentation of how his music evolved over the course of a tour, often with young untried musicians and unfamiliar

Miles feels the heat at a live performance. 1960

material. Apart from wire recordings and tapes of radio broadcasts, there were no live records of Miles Davis in performance.

That changed in 1961. Miles's last major engagements with John Coltrane had been a European tour supported by Norman Granz's "Jazz at the Philharmonic". Cannonball Adderley had already left the group, and Coltrane was anxious to follow him. Bill Evans was already causing a stir with his trio. Much as he lamented their departure, nearly breaking down on stage as he announced Coltrane's departure, Miles generously supported all three, talking enthusiastically about their work to journalists and booking agents. He bought Coltrane a soprano saxophone, an instrument at that time virtually ignored by jazz musicians, but like his own revival of the flugelhorn destined to be imitated by a huge number of tenor saxophonists. As if to further demonstrate his unwillingness to let Coltrane go, he also recalled him to play on the title track of his next studio record *Some Day My Prince Will Come*, a performance that greatly influenced the saxophonist's own later transformation - or subversion - of sentimental Broadway songs. Miles himself had heard the Disney song played by Bill Evans and his trio, with whom he shared a bill at the Village Vanguard on his return from Europe.

At this time, Miles was experimenting with a new line-up. He had briefly recruited Sonny Stitt, who was seen by many, including Bird himself, as another of Charlie Parker's apostolic successors, but who had tried to evade the comparison by giving up alto saxophone in favour of tenor. He was clearly not the right choice, perhaps because he was too reminiscent of Parker, but Miles's next choice was even more unexpected. In place of the complex, introverted Coltrane, he recruited Hank Mobley, creator of a series of solid, deceptively unsophisticated hard bop albums on Blue Note. The critics and audiences who'd consistently underrated Mobley were surprised, but Miles's instincts, as ever, were proved exactly right.

The proof lies in a body of work that was only made publicly available in 2003. After Miles's death, Columbia embarked on an ambitious and very lucrative re-issue programme, repackaging his classic albums, but also releasing some of the many hours of tape held in the company's vaults.

To a degree, this reflected Miles's unusual working methods of the late 1960s and 1970s, when he liked to tape long, undifferentiated sections of music in studio and then leave it to producer/engineer Teo Macero to edit and assemble a satisfying album from the results. This is essentially how *In a Silent Way, Bitches Brew* and *Jack Johnson* were created. However, Columbia also held a substantial number of live tapes.

Some of the quintet's French and Scandinavian concerts had been bootlegged or taped by radio stations and there is a substantial, semi-official documentation of the spring 1960 tour. These records offer a superb insight into how Miles and his sidemen tackled similar material over different nights, how radically but also tentatively Miles was moving towards a new sound, once again tougher, "blacker" and, thanks to Wynton Kelly's presence in the group, more obviously grounded in the blues.

Whether Miles or Columbia had had a chance to hear any of the Scandinavian tapes (now available on the Dragon label and elsewhere) they would have been impressed by the clarity and fidelity of the recordings, as well as by their musical content. Jazz in its essence is a live, exploratory art. Before the advent of the LP era, there was a considerable gap between studio playing and the extended improvisations of a live date. The advent of 12" records narrowed it, but Miles was conscious that even his own open-ended approach - which reached an apotheosis on *Kind of Blue* - still involved a safety net. His later practice was to turn the studio into a kind of nightclub, having his players jam freely for long periods on very basic material and seeing what would emerge.

To a degree, the method was fixed in his mind by what happened at a small San Francisco club on April 21 and 22 1961. Though less well known in recent years than a later date - December 1965 - with a different group at the Plugged Nickel club in Chicago, the so-called *Complete Blackhawk Sessions* are by far the most important of the posthumous Miles Davis reissues and complete editions. There is some controversy among jazz fans and writers as to the merits of releasing extra material from recording dates and live events. The increased duration of CD allows the inclusion of tracks omitted on first release, often it has to be said, tracks that were considered

Miles playing at Birdland. 1949

sub-standard by the artists and producer at the time. Such fragments are, however, ardently collected and studied. Even Charlie Parker's abandoned "takes" and breakdowns yield insights into his work, and the same is true of Miles's San Francisco residency.

Even without the presence of John Coltrane, *Friday Night at the Blackhawk* and *Saturday Night at the Blackhawk,* as the two original LPs were labelled, are far more coherent and compelling than the group's stilted work on *Some Day My Prince Will Come.* Coltrane had walked into that session and picked up exactly where he left off, playing a brilliant solo on the title track after the merest glance at the chords, and reprising some of his best work from the *Kind of Blue* sessions on "Teo", an open-ended, Spanish-tinged piece in three-quarter time dedicated to producer Teo Macero, who was playing an ever more important part in Miles's musical life.

There are rhythmic oddities on the original release, not because the rhythm section couldn't keep time - drummer Jimmy Cobb was particularly sensitive to this charge - but because Miles and Teo edited together preferred segments of different performances. There was a considerable overlap of material, even though just two sets were taped on each of the two nights recorded. Miles habitually failed to turn up for final sets, or simply walked off the stand after a couple of numbers. He may have been in physical pain from the arthritis caused by sickle cell, or he may simply have become disgusted at the behaviour of non-listening drinkers in the clubs where he played. He wasn't prepared to make an exception for the Blackhawk, which for all its shabbiness was a music-lovers' spot which enjoined silence and serious listening.

The first revelation of the *Complete Blackhawk Sessions,* released in 2003, lies in hearing the original performances intact, unedited and in the actual order of playing. More important, though, is how thoroughly they interrogate a received consensus about Miles and his music. Even though he and the group were aware that microphones and recording equipment were present, this was still a club date and not a studio recording, and therefore a truer reflection of his musical thinking than the slightly wooden March dates that yielded *Some Day My Prince Will Come.*

Sonny Rollins

One cliche seems immediately and perversely confirmed. Miles makes a complete hash of his entry on Sonny Rollins's fast bebop theme "Oleo", suggesting that bop really wasn't his metier. But where is Miles the "minimalist", the soft-voiced and at times quasi-classical player who rarely stepped out of the middle register and eschewed the high-wire antics of Dizzy Gillespie? The Blackhawk sessions find him playing faster, louder, higher and with a more aggressive edge than had ever been heard on record before. Anyone who only knew Miles from *Kind of Blue*'s abstract nocturnes would not have credited that the player on "Bye Bye Blackbird", "On Green Dolphin Street" and even on the lovely "Fran-dance" was the same artist. Even with the Harmon mute in place, he sounds different, though anyone who had listened with care to *L'ascenseur pour l'echafaud* would have shared Miles's recognition that he could convey violence and anger on muted trumpet every bit as easily as he could project a limpid beauty on the open horn.

Miles had rarely been associated with the blues, but the San Francisco performances are steeped in Blues form. Here, much of the credit must go to Wynton Kelly, who is the real hero of the Blackhawk albums. His accompaniments are precise, energising and rarely far from blues tonality. He even takes an unaccompanied spot on "Love, I've Found You". Hank Mobley's solos might seem modest, but only compared to John Coltrane's endless spiritual peregrinations; heard on their own terms, they are subtle, funky and effortlessly to the point. They also fit Miles's purpose perfectly, foils to his slashing, moody solos.

Had the Blackhawk sessions been better known during Miles's lifetime, they might have helped inoculate criticism against some of the absurd generalities that attach to Miles's reputation. Their relative obscurity is largely circumstantial. In planning their sumptuous reissue programme after his death Columbia, gave more weight to the 1965 Plugged Nickel sessions, which are aesthetically smoother but not necessarily superior. Even at the time of release, the Blackhawk tapes were overtaken by events.

There could hardly be a greater geographical and physical contrast than between the Blackhawk - which owner Guido Caccienti cheerfully, indeed proudly, admitted was a slum - and the location of Miles's next major public appearance. One of the reasons Columbia were slow to market the Blackhawk LPs was that on May 19 1961 Miles, his quintet, and the Gil Evans orchestra performed and were recorded at the most prestigious classical music venue in New York City. The resulting album *Miles Davis at the Carnegie Hall* is his only live record in the company of Gil Evans's orchestra. It was a benefit event for the African Research Foundation, a circumstance that prompted a curiously misguided pro-African protest by Miles's old colleague, drummer Max Roach, who was highly politicised at the time. Despite his interruption, the evening was a triumph and Miles's playing on "Teo" and "Oleo" (both staples of the time and both prominent on the Blackhawk set-list) and on big-band arrangements of "So What", "New Rhumba" and "The Meaning of the Blues" is exemplary. Upset but also inspired he returned to the stage and played with real fire.

His anger wasn't just of the moment, and not merely sparked by Roach's intervention. At the cusp of the 60s, Miles might seem to have been on top of the world, but as ever he was to reflect the decade's ambiguities and face further problems of his own.

The Prince of Darkness

One might have expected Miles Davis to go into 1962 energised and confident. He led a poll-winning group - now a sextet again with trombonist J.J. Johnson - commanded substantial booking fees and, thanks to Prestige and Columbia in parallel, had built up a substantial catalogue of recordings. Unfortunately, though, Miles's group was not only vulnerable to the personal vicissitudes of its members; it was also a victim of its own success. Paul Chambers continued to have problems, as did Red Garland and Philly Joe Jones, who made occasional returns to the group when regular members Wynton Kelly and Jimmy Cobb were unavailable. Sonny Rollins briefly rejoined but did not consider the possibility of a permanent engagement when Hank Mobley decided to move on. Like the others, Rollins was developing an independent career as a leader. Membership of Miles's group was a guarantee of celebrity in the small world of jazz, but Miles was also an exacting and volatile leader who liked things done his way and was not usually interested in allowing his musicians to develop their own ideas. Over the next two years, Miles would experiment with three different tenor saxophonists and with dramatic changes in his rhythm section.

There were other pressures. Success left him open to litigation and when he was obliged to cancel dates - sometimes through his own ill health, but more often thanks to the unprofessionalism of his sidemen - he was sued for loss of earnings. Though by no means as politically volatile as Max Roach, Miles was considered too unpredictable and rebarbative a personality to represent the USA abroad, as he had more than a decade earlier at the 1949 Paris Jazz Fair. While musicians as diverse as Dave Brubeck, Herbie Mann and Dizzy Gillespie made government-funded tours of the

Wayne Shorter

Middle East as part of the State Department's and CIA's effort to project America as a colour-blind culture which respected the contribution of its racial minorities, Miles was consistently overlooked, and seethed on the sidelines. He had experimented with multi-racial groups for purely musical reasons and it must have galled him intensely to see Gillespie (always a more militant, even separatist figure) breaking new audiences abroad with a cosmetically chequered line-up.

The year also brought a personal tragedy. Miles's father died suddenly. He had suffered injuries in a level-crossing accident that had left him unable to practice well short of retirement age, and while he had no immediate financial worries, his disability brought a loss of esteem. Whatever conflicts he had had with his father, Miles respected him and was grieved that they had not been fully reconciled. Cleo Davis died two years later, and Miles found a reason not to be at the funeral.

His parents' decline sourly underscored Miles's own problems. As those who worked with him attest, he was in constant pain at this time, and resorted to cocaine, alcohol and a cocktail of prescription drugs to get through his work schedule. His moods were volatile but often streaked with pessimism. Not since 1953 had he recorded so little. He didn't enter a recording studio before July and only then for the desultory *Quiet Night* sessions, which required padding out at a later date. The following month he made three tracks with singer Bob Dorough, his first recording with a vocalist since a May 1950 session for singer Sarah Vaughan. These are inconsequential tracks, though one of them would later appear - bafflingly - on the 1967 album *Sorcerer*, but they're important for a first glimpse in Miles's ranks of the 28 year old Wayne Shorter.

It was to be another two years before the brilliant tenor saxophonist became a permanent member of what most agree was Miles's greatest ever group. In the interim, Miles recruited the strong-voiced George Coleman and more briefly alto player Frank Strozier and another tenor and soprano specialist Sam Rivers, who was probably too avant-garde and only played with the group for a couple of months in the summer of 1964.

Strozier wasn't the only last-minute call Miles had to make on his arrival in California at the beginning of 1963 after another thin period in the studios. Chambers and Kelly had gone; Cobb was soon to follow. Miles was obliged to use local players like Victor Feldman, a British-born pianist and vibraharpist and drummer Frank Butler, but he also secured the services of bassist Ron Carter, a disciple of Paul Chambers and probably the only musician on the scene blessed with the same sure tone, subtle rhythmic sense and musical vision. Like Hank Mobley before him, Coleman is a deceptive player, whose muscularity of delivery camouflages a formidable harmonic understanding. His tenure with Miles was brief but effective and the group's performances at the Antibes Festival in late July 1963 are as much a showcase for the saxophonist as for the leader.

The MC Andre Francis makes a particularly warm introduction to "*le jeune Tony Williams a la batterie . . . il a dix-sept ans*". Miles had made a tentative return to the studio earlier in the spring with his West Coast pick-up band. Though some of the material did find its way on to his next record *Seven Steps to Heaven*, the tracks with Feldman, Carter and Butler, and even those with Coleman added, are eclipsed by the material recorded a month later in New York where Coleman and Carter were joined by pianist Herbie Hancock and the 17 year old prodigy Williams, who was still technically under age for most club licenses and required chaperoning by the stable and sober Ron Carter. The Los Angeles tracks are bland in the extreme and Miles surprised critics and audiences by including two very old jazz standards, "Basin Street Blues" and "Baby, Won't You Please Come Home", a clear sign of how deeply rooted in the past he was, but a confusing gesture for those who saw him as the great innovator. The title tune, "Seven Steps to Heaven", was re-recorded by the new group, but the issued album still sounds bitty and unfinished and some of Miles's playing on the Californian sessions drifts close to self-parody.

The new group, though, was pushing Miles in new directions. Hancock, Carter and Williams were initially very disciplined when playing behind the leader, but clearly felt comfortable enough to experiment when Coleman was soloing, particularly when his use of rhythm changes and altered harmonics called for unorthodox accompaniment. Young and fresh, the new rhythm section was capable of brilliant orthodoxy but also of extremely inventive variations on basic jazz changes and metres. Gradually, this began to have an effect on the trumpeter as well. Having brought his modal approach to a high pitch on *Kind of Blue*, Miles began to experiment with a greater degree of chromaticism in his solos, incorporating notes which did not belong in the scale he was ostensibly using, taking a less functional, more abstract approach to harmony.

It's significant that, initially at least, the band was only documented in live performance and playing what must have looked on paper like shop-soiled material: nothing quite as old as "Basin Street Blues" but standard tunes like "Autumn Leaves", "Stella By Starlight", "My Funny Valentine", as well as his own now very familiar "So What" and "All Blues". Aware that his new approach was still unfamiliar, possibly even alien, Miles didn't want to compound the unfamiliarity by playing brand new material. Club and concert performances - and there are records of the group from Philharmonic Hall, New York (February, with Coleman on tenor saxophone), Tokyo (July, with Rivers) and Berlin (autumn, with Shorter) - allowed him to stretch out and experiment with his new rhythm section and new playing style. Also quite simply, his engagement diary was too full to consider studio work as well. After a period of creative stasis, Miles was enjoying his work again.

Sometimes, he and they got it wrong. *Four and More,* an LP of faster numbers from the Philharmonic Hall concert, is strained and patchy. And yet the slower numbers, collected on a separate album called *My Funny Valentine* after its finest track, are uniformly remarkable. Miles's solo on the title track is unexpectedly radical, full of tension and drama, and in contrast to the quartet version made for Prestige in October 1956, played on open horn rather than with the Harmon. Miles's articulation has never sounded better, ironically at the moment when his playing moves inexorably into unfamiliar terrain. Similarly "Stella By Starlight" acquires a troubling, almost discursive quality, as if Miles were deconstructing the original song rather than merely playing variations on its melody or changes. *My Funny Valentine* vies with *Miles Davis in Europe* for supremacy at this period. The record of his appearance at Juan-les-Pins for the Antibes Festival, a full seven months before the Philharmonic Hall benefit, is marked by the brashness and youthful intensity of a rhythm section still not used to playing behind Miles. The later date documents a more settled and confident, but also less playful interaction. Arguably, too, the assassination of John F Kennedy in November 1963 cast its shadow. Miles admired the handsome young president and his beautiful wife, believing that he represented a genuine possibility of breakthrough for racial equality in America. He unofficially dedicated the Philharmonic Hall concert - actually a benefit for various pressure groups - to the murdered president.

In Antibes, the cloud of Dallas still hadn't passed over the sun. Miles's muted solo on "Autumn Leaves" is spacious and unpredictable, alternating areas of minimum activity with incredibly dense passages; somewhat like his playing at the Blackhawk club, but with infinitely more dramatic tension. Elsewhere, he played familiar pieces at nearly double the original tempo, notably the warhorse "Milestones", here turned into the kind of thoroughbred Miles admired, and the even more venerable "Walkin'", which has switched to a delightful and delighted canter. Williams's vivid drumming and Carter's intense, ringing tone are integral to the performance. Hancock and Coleman play more conventionally, but almost as if they are providing a foil the better to show off the radical new style.

After taking Sam Rivers on what turned out to be a triumphant visit to Japan, Miles eventually managed to prise Wayne Shorter away from the Jazz Messengers, which at the time was the only comparably high-profile group in jazz, albeit of a more conservative stamp. Any residual misgivings the saxophonist may have had were overcome by Miles's oblique philosophy. In return Miles had brought on board a formidable young composer. Over the next five years, Shorter not only emerged as a significant collaborator in the development of Miles's new "time - no changes" approach he also supplied the group with some of its most distinctive material: the delightful, blues-based "Footprints", "Nefertiti", "The Fall" and "Prince of Darkness" (which became Miles's alter-ego). For the first time, Miles seemed content to delegate specific compositional tasks to his sidemen, or to give them

Miles sticks his tongue out at the audience during a performance. 1965

joint credit as he did on "Eighty-One" on the *ESP* album. It's a deceptive situation because in doing so he retained, possibly even increased - his overall control of the music.

"Time - no changes" referred to Miles's decision to abandon chordal sequences in favour of an open-form approach with an agreed pulse but nothing like the song-based chorus form that had dominated jazz hitherto. In practice, the rhythm section responded to the soloists' free-form improvisations rather than supplying a harmonic and rhythmic foundation.The method was the logical extension of what Miles had been been doing since *L'ascenseur pour l'echafaud*. It suited Shorter's unpredictable, asymmetrical delivery every bit as well.

Miles had fallen out with Teo Macero over the release of *Quiet Nights* and had not discussed *In Europe, Four and More* or *My Funny Valentine* with his latest creative alter ego. The rift was still not healed in January 1965, when Miles took the new group into the studio for the first time. Not too much should be inferred from his decision to record in San Francisco rather than New York. He already had an engagement at The Hungry i club and the critical factor was probably that rather than a desire to spite Macero by working with Columbia's West Coast operation.

The new album was called *E.S.P.*, after one of Wayne Shorter's compositions, which might seem a strange choice given that ESP-Disk was the New York label responsible for putting out the kind of avant-garde free jazz - the music of Albert Ayler   - which Miles professed to dislike. Parts of his own record might almost have acquired that same label. Having virtually abandoned chords and song-forms in favour of abstract collages of melodic fragments, Miles seemed to be drifting in the direction of playing "out", as the current parlance had it.

Ironically, *E.S.P.* is also the first record on which Miles seems to be flirting with rock. "Eighty-One" has a strong backbeat, and the kind of regular, repetitive bass line and percussion that was characteristic of funk, and still considered somewhat *infra dig* in jazz. Any suggestion that Miles only began to explore a rock idiom on 1969's *Bitches Brew* misses the mark by a good four years. "Eighty-One" is the only track on the album that goes in this direction, though other tracks exploit Carter's and Williams's ability to infuse a very regular 4/4 beat with infinite subtlety.

Like "Eighty-One", the closing "Mood" is jointly credited to Miles and his bassist. "R.J." is Carter's alone, "E.S.P." and "Iris" are Shorter compositions, while "Little One" offers an earnest of Herbie Hancock's writing skills. Miles claims just one sole credit, and that is for the fast, edgy

"Agitation", which looks forward to the clangorous open-form jams that formed the basic material of his controversial late 60s, early 70s albums.

Even more than on the studio version, the live versions of "Agitation" taped at the Plugged Nickel in December of 1965 find him moving in this direction. At this period it seems less relevant to talk about Miles's trumpet sound than about the overall impact of the group. He was gradually breaking down the familiar relationships of theme-and-variations, soloist and accompaniment in favour of a textural and episodic approach. In it, he anticipates the "nobody solos and everybody solos all of the time" philosophy of Shorter's next band Weather Report and to an extent the deconstruction of song form his young friend Prince was striving for on albums like 1986's *Sign 'O' The Times*.

After the January 1965 sessions in Los Angeles, Miles dropped out of sight for much of the year. The osteological degeneration in his hip had advanced so far that a replacement was required. Miles spent the late spring and summer in hospital, first undergoing bone grafts and then the wholesale replacement of the hip joint with a plastic prosthesis. The circumstances of the second operation recall how Miles's voice was permanently damaged. Despite having been warned to rest, he discharged himself from hospital and undid the initial surgical work in a serious fall at home. He didn't play live again until November 1965. Even a month later at the Plugged Nickel he sounds tired and lacking in fire, ceding the spotlight to the burgeoning Shorter.

Illness and inactivity can sometimes be a spur to renewed creativity. One of the guests at Miles's and Frances's party for Robert Kennedy had been Bob Dylan who in 1966 was sidelined by a much-mythologised motorcycle accident. Surviving not only a potentially serious neck injury but a tidal wave of media rumours, Dylan returned a very different artist. At the start of 1966, Miles Davis seemed less resilient than that. As he turned 40 and became a grandfather, he seemed to be struggling to keep pace with deep, almost seismic changes in the music business. Jazz was steadily losing ground to pop and rock. Indeed, the only jazz musicians who were thriving were Dave Brubeck, who had cornered a preppy college market, and the saxophonist Charles Lloyd, who moved to Atlantic Records in 1966 with a

Herbie Hancock

young quartet including future Miles associates Keith Jarrett on piano and Jack DeJohnette on drums and playing a brand of jazz that incorporated rock and elements of psychedelia.

Lloyd and Miles would cross paths, but for the moment the trumpeter seemed content to consolidate his abstract approach, making another five albums with the Shorter/Hancock/Carter/Williams quintet, together with enough studio material for two further compilations. Released in 1966 and 1967 *Miles Smiles, The Sorcerer* and *Nefertiti* continue the pattern established by *E.S.P.* Or rather they extend it, since Miles has no compositional credits at all on the latter two records. He remains in powerful command of the music nonetheless. As Herbie Hancock, one of the two main designated composers put it: "I guess what he wanted to go for was the core of the music . . . a composition is an example of a conception, so Miles, rather than play the composition, he wants to play the conception that the composition comes from . . . That's why you hear melody fragments and you kind of hear the momentum and the sound of the tune somewhere . . ." - as good a description of the impression of these albums as can be imagined.

Some of the tunes are very good indeed. Band members were frustrated that in concert and in clubs Miles shrewdly insisted on playing old favourites like "Milestones", "Round About Midnight", "So What", rather than the new tunes the band was creating in studio. Shorter's "Footprints" on *Miles Smiles* is a modern jazz classic, rooted in the blues but with a strongly contemporary feel in the bass line and in Tony Williams' exuberantly disciplined and subtly free-form drumming. Hancock's "Gingerbread Boy" is equally delightful, and the same album features a fine arrangement of Eddie Harris's soul-jazz favourite "Freedom Jazz Dance". On the later records, as the titles perhaps suggest, the mood is more sombre. *Nefertiti* seems dourly "experimental" and inward-looking, while *The Sorcerer,* recorded a month earlier in May 1967, plays like a self-conscious expression of Miles's tender-aggressive ego: "The Prince of Darkness".

In his autobiography, he remembers a dinner party in Chicago where he was playing an engagement. Present at it were journalist Marc Crawford, who was writing a major profile of Miles for *Ebony* magazine, Miles's sister Dorothy Davis, and also his mother, towards the end of her life. She mentions Miles's increasingly abrasive and diffident public persona, a manner which made a title like *Miles Smiles* seem more than ironic. Why not repay the public's loyalty and affection with a gentler demeanour. "I said, 'What do you want me to be, an Uncle Tom?' She looked at me real hard for a minute and then she said, 'If I ever hear about you tomming, I'll come and kill you myself'." It's a further reminder that the oedipal strain in Miles Davis's character had complex roots. With his father and mother gone, other friends lost to chance, close relationships strained to breaking, who he chose to surround himself with was almost as important to Miles as the music he made.

Directions in Music

The mournful woman in the trumpeter's shadow on the cover of *Friday/Saturday at the Blackhawk* is Frances Taylor Davis. At a time when most record labels insisted on putting pretty white girls on the cover of jazz records, cheesecake images that often jarred with the musical content, Miles had "started demanding that Columbia use black women on my album covers". Frances had already appeared on the front of *Some Day My Prince Will Come,* which included the theme "Pfrancing" inspired by her. She figured again (with Miles) on *E.S.P.* but within days of being photographed for that record she walked out, ending a passionate but stormy (and ultimately violent) relationship and breaking up the seemingly happy family home in that converted Russian Orthodox church on West 77th Street.

Over the next two and a half years, the course of Miles's romantic life could be traced by his cover art. His relationship with the beautiful actress Cicely Tyson resulted in her appearance on the cover of *Sorcerer* in 1967; their affair resumed some years later and she became Miles's third wife, only divorcing him two years before his death. After Miles's divorce from Frances was finalised in February 1968, he fell in love with singer Betty Mabry, the "Mademoiselle Mabry" celebrated on his next album *Filles de Kilimanjaro* and on whose cover she appears. They were married later that year, and separated twelve months later, apparently because Betty - who continued to use her married surname for the rest of her career, despite its similarity to Bette Davis - had an affair with rock guitarist Jimi Hendrix. A subsequent relationship with Marguerite Eskridge, who was riding in Miles's Ferrari at the time of the shooting incident, led to her appearance on the cover of *At the Fillmore.* They had a son together, Erin, his fourth and last child.

Despite the addition to his family, people were leaving Miles. In the later 60s, his love life was more turbulent than at any time since his romance with Juliette Greco. Trusted musicians had used the cachet of playing in his band to promote their solo careers. He had a further violent falling-out with drummer Max Roach. His mother and father had passed on, and in July 1967 John Coltrane succumbed to liver cancer, having continued to work right to the end.

Miles's reaction to his old colleague's passing was characteristically terse and pungent, but also more than personal: "it f***ed up everyone. . . . His death created chaos in the 'free thing' because he was its leader. He was like Bird to all those musicians who considered themselves 'out' - you know, 'free', out in space: he was like a god to them". How literally that last phrase might be taken can be gauged from the existence in San Francisco of the Saint John Coltrane African Orthodox Church, a tiny storefront communion which regards Trane's extended improvisations as actual routes to spiritual transcendence. His immediate musical legacy, fragmented and problematic, was also given a strong religious resonance when tenor saxophonist Albert Ayler, who played at Coltrane's funeral, located himself and fellow saxophonist Pharoah Sanders in a new jazz Trinity: "Tranc was the Father, Pharoah is the Son, and I am the Holy Ghost".

Miles was basically hostile to the "free thing", but in his autobiography he recognises that it was part of a wider movement that held black revolutionary pride and a new social and political consciousness among young whites in the same uneasy gravitational field. Coltrane's death might have bequeathed him automatic leadership had the jazz scene in 1967 been less fragmented. The only other claimants were either too derivative (Sanders), too eccentric (Ayler and alto saxophonist Ornette Coleman) or too musically obdurate (pianist Cecil Taylor). And besides, jazz's status as the natural vehicle of cultural alienation and social protest was being challenged by the unstoppable rise of rock.

Just over a decade after Elvis Presley's emergence, rock was firmly in the saddle, offering the uniquely satisfying combination of rebellion and profit. It had even established a beachhead at Columbia Records, where

Betty Mabry and Miles Davis arrive at the funeral of Jimi Hendrix. 1970

in 1966 Clive Davis (no relation) had been appointed vice-president and had begun to sign up rock and pop artists with budgets that immediately threatened Miles's position. He had a clear choice. Either follow the avant-garde route and risk a steady marginalisation, or else attempt to capture

some of the energy (and audience) of the new music.

To anyone with even a passing knowledge of rock history, a title like *Live at the Fillmore* suggests how much his demographic had shifted since those live sets from the Blackhawk and Plugged Nickel and even Carnegie Hall. In addition to introducing him to Jimi Hendrix and Sly

Stone, two important influences on his later style, Betty Mabry also began to encourage Miles to abandon the dark Italian suits, crisp white shirts and ties that had been his usual stage clothing and experiment with a funkier look. Though for a time his new look was mainly reserved for photo shoots, from here until the end of his life Miles began to dress ever more extravagantly. In the 80s he would appear on stage in bright silk harem pants, white vest and cropped bomber jacket, with a sailor's cap covering the wig he adopted to cover his prematurely thinning hair. For the time being, though, Miles was for once sartorially behind the times. In preferring a relatively conventional presentation, he distanced himself somewhat from the jeans and tie-dye look of young, white, hippy rock bands, but also more significantly from the separatist flamboyance of the avant-garde, whether it was Ornette Coleman's home-made clothes or the dashikis and kaftans favoured by other performers.

If the look developed slowly, the music was progressing in a series of evolutionary jumps. If, for the time being, Miles and his group still looked like a jazz group of the 1950s, there was no doubt that Miles had made creative allegiance with the younger rock, pop and soul acts. He was increasingly dismissive of "jazz" as a term, partly because he found it racially and culturally demeaning, but also because in straightforward business terms jazz was becoming a poorly invested ghetto, certainly at Columbia.

If there is a single, clear indication of his willingness to embrace and assimilate a new idiom to his own musical vision, it is his decision to incorporate electric instruments in the group, and not just electric keyboards and basses but the totemic instrument of rock, the electric guitar. To that extent, the sessions of December 4 and 28 1967 - the very cusp of what became the counterculture's signature year - are particularly significant. The two long tracks recorded on those sessions were only released much later - "Circle in the Round" on the LP of that name in 1979, towards the end of Miles's "retirement", and "Water on the Pond" - but what is striking about them is the change in the group sound. Herbie Hancock plays celeste on the first track, electric piano and clavinet on the second. Miles himself also plays chimes and bells, prefiguring a time in the 1970s when he played more organ than trumpet. Finally, the quintet is augmented for the first time. A second drummer - unidentified - can be heard faintly during "Water on the Pond" but more significant is the addition of a guitarist.

Joe Beck does little more than double Ron Carter's bass lines, adding "bottom", extra fullness, to the group, but in his modest way he was the forerunner to a line of guitarists - Larry Coryell, Pete Cosey, Reggie Lucas, Dominique Gaumont, John McLaughlin - who would occupy a far more prominent position in future line-ups. It's clear that Miles wasn't just experimenting randomly, or letting Beck merely "sit in". When the quintet went back into the studio in January 1968, Bucky Pizzarelli briefly joined the group on "Fun" (released on the compilation *Directions*); a week later and again in February, George Benson was added to the strength for three tracks, all of which later appeared on *Circle in the Round*.

Significantly, none of these recordings was slated for immediate release. In future years, Columbia would be grateful to have a body of unissued work in the vault, to cover Miles's period of inactivity; he himself would have recognised that they were sketchy essays rather than finished work. The quintet continued to recorded steadily through the summer of 1967, completing the *Sorcerer* and *Nefertiti* sessions, but also taping enough additional material for a further album, *Water Babies,* released later and rounded out with tracks from November 1968. An exhaustive boxed set *Miles Davis Quintet: 1965-1968* underlines just how much time his musicians spent in Columbia's 30th Street Studios. It also confirms an impression that is evident even on the released albums: that the group was almost self-consciously pursuing novelty, pushing against a kind of creative inertia that threatened to stall Mile's most creative unit. The complexity of the music almost seems to function as a bulwark against the kind open, melodic, backbeat-driven pop that surrounded everyone that year and in which the players - Miles and Hancock certainly - were deeply interested, albeit contrary to all natural instinct.

Another, older instinct was resurfacing in Miles's creative life, coupled to the revival of an older creative relationship. For a period, Miles had relied on compositions by his sidemen - Shorter in particular - but by the beginning of 1968 he had started to write again. Significantly, this coincided with a further Gil Evans collaboration, an unissued track apparently called "Falling Water" and apparently featuring Hawaiian guitar! - and with Evans' renewed role as a kind of secret sharer, part-arranger, part-sounding board, part-musical tutor. Much has been made over the years, not least by Macero himself, of producer Teo Macero's creative input into Miles's records at this period. The reality is that Macero was a fine engineer and brilliant editor, with ongoing musical aspirations of his own. There is no evidence - indeed, evidence to the contrary - that Miles ever ceded artistic responsibility to him. The opposite is true of Gil Evans, who remained a powerful influence and seems to have helped clear away the rather clotted, introverted thinking of *Sorcerer* and *Nefertiti*. (The additional oddity of *Sorcerer* was the inclusion of a vocal track, "Nothing Like You", made in 1962 with Bob Dorough and nothing like Miles's more recent music.) Evans was first and foremost a communicator and at a time when Miles's market position was in some doubt, accessibility was a major issue.

Ian Carr shrewdly detects a parallelism between the albums Miles made in the period 1958-1961 and those he made over exactly the same span a decade later. Two mournful masterpieces ten years apart: *Kind of Blue* and *In a Silent Way*, a very deliberate step away from jazz sources with *Sketches of Spain* and *Bitches Brew*, the shaky *Some Day My Prince Will Come* echoed in two shambolic live records *Black Beauty* and *At Fillmore,* and finally a more contentious connection between the brilliant live records of 1961 *Friday/Saturday at the Blackhawk* and the Carnegie Hall concert and the boiling fury of *Live-Evil*. Carr also includes *Jack Johnson* in the final pairing, though as we'll see its more obvious forerunner in creative terms is the *L'Ascenseur pour l'echafaud* soundtrack. It's a persuasive argument, and also confirmation that far from being committed to change in a straight line, Miles's career seemed to evolve in long loops, with the same creative dilemmas, the same personnel issues confronted afresh.

The first fruits of his return to composition appeared on *Miles in the Sky*, mostly recorded in May 1968. The word "transitional" is applicable to so much of Miles's work as to have become almost meaningless, but here one senses an artist and a group caught between two directions. That's symbolised in Herbie Hancock's and Ron Carter's use of both electric and acoustic instruments on the session. What's unambiguous on the record is Miles's growing attraction to the immediacy of rock, a fascination already evident on *E.S.P.*'s "Eighty-One", but not fully developed there. His two compositions open and close the album. The lead-off track, "Stuff", abandons the rhythmic complexities of the two previous albums in favour of a driving rock beat in which Hancock, Carter and Williams rarely waver from the basic count. There is, however, nothing straightforward about Miles's theme statement and solo. The former is long, groping, almost distressing in its deliberate incoherence. The solo that follows is a clever indication that the chaotic melody is planned and deliberate. It's also much less important than the original statement, almost an elaborate footnote. So, too, are the solos by Shorter, Hancock and Williams.

If the drummer seemed to have been relegated to a cruder, less creative role - an understandable but incorrect assumption - he was rewarded as a composer with the inclusion of his own "Black Comedy", a minimal structure that does little more than set up the kind of abstract soloing Miles and the quintet had pioneered earlier in the decade. It's also an acoustic piece. The third track of the set, actually taken from an earlier session (January 1968), is the only one to feature guitarist George Benson. The final item is Miles's other composition, "Country Son", a curiously structured minor-key idea that seems to throw together disparate elements of the group's recent thinking - some straight jazz, a hint of slow blues-rock, a measure of abstraction in Miles's strange solo - and makes them work, or very nearly. The other odd thing about the track is Miles's muted sound; instead of his trademark adapted Harmon, he uses a straight mute and a cleaner sonority, albeit deployed in all manner of unusual trills, smears and growls. Here, the "transitional" label is almost unavoidable, but it seems an odd gesture to end the album with a piece that so obviously points back as well as forward, instead of with "Stuff", which is unambiguously new.

It's potentially misleading to talk about "solos" on *Miles in the Sky*. The word implies a more conventional structure of themes and variations, functional ensembles interspersed with individual features. Miles's new direction was closer to the ideal espoused in Weather Report: "Nobody solos and everybody solos all of the time". What Miles sought was a unified group sound in which the old hierarchies of material and instrumental elements were being overturned. Quite how thoroughly only became evident over the next twelve months and the next three Miles Davis albums.

Not for the first time, Miles found himself having to break in a new rhythm section. Not for the first time, he turned contingency to creative profit. Like Red Garland, Bill Evans, John Coltrane and even the loyal Philly Joe Jones before them, Hancock, Carter and Williams wanted to develop their own careers. Now 23, the drummer had already made records as leader for Blue Note and was anxious to pursue the fiery, rock-inspired style that led to the formation (with two other Miles alumni) of Lifetime in 1969. By his own account, Carter was tired of incessant touring, but he also had a solo career to follow and, as a first-call bass player, enough work to keep him busy seven days a week. The circumstances of Hancock's actual departure were more mysterious - he took ill on honeymoon - but he had the additional motivation of feeling marginalised as a composer by Shorter and, once Miles started to write again, by the leader as well.

The next quintet album, *Filles de Kilimanjaro,* was actually made by two different groups. Three of the numbers were recorded in June 1968 by the existing group in its electronic incarnation, the remaining two by a new lineup, which included Chick Corea on electric piano and with him a new bass player as well. Miles had courted controversy in the late 40s by recruiting white players for his nonet. Now he took this a step further, for Carter's replacement Dave Holland was not only white but an Englishman, whom Miles had seen playing while on vacation in London and recruited on the spot. Hancock was to return in November for a session that contributed further tracks to the *Directions,* and *Water Babies* albums, and in February 1969 for what were to be the *In a Silent Way* sessions; in future, too, he would reappear from time to time, particularly when the music called for two keyboard players. That also opened the way for the later inclusion of the brilliant Austrian emigre Joe Zawinul, who later founded Weather Report with Wayne Shorter; organist Larry Young, who was a charter member of Williams's Lifetime trio; and the brilliant young pianist Keith Jarrett, who was a member of saxophonist Charles Lloyd's quartet, a group Miles would frequently encounter in his new rock incarnation.

There is a slight irony in the recruitment of Corea and Jarrett to an electric group in that both men showed a marked reluctance to play electronic instruments, initially only in the case of Corea, who went on to form his own fusion group Return to Forever, but a lifelong antipathy in Jarrett's case, and it's testimony to Miles's powers of persuasion that he convinced him. For the moment, though, the piano chair was Corea's and Miles enjoyed the hard, percussive bass notes and swirling clusters that were available on the Fender Rhodes instrument. He himself later explored similar sonorities on electric organ.

Corea's first studio appearance with the group yielded what became the opening track on *Filles de Kilimanjaro.* "Frelon Brun" - or "Brown Hornet" - is a taut, rock motif with an unmistakably African time-feel. Piano and bass reinforce one another, as guitar and bass had on previous sessions, while horns and drums surge to and fro in a new, Africanised variant of the old call-and-response structure of the blues, which Miles and Gil Evans had adapted so brilliantly on *Miles Ahead* and *Porgy & Bess.* It's no surprise to learn that Evans was once again to play the grey eminence, though he preferred to liken his role to midwifery. The other piece recorded at the September 24 1968 session is Miles's love poem to Betty, "Mademoiselle Mabry". Interestingly, and in a way that would have appealed to the classicist in Corea, the rhythm section part is completely composed rather than merely indicating the chord changes and metre, with no formally written part for the horns. Even as an evolution of the group's practice on *Sorcerer, Nefertiti* and *Miles in the Sky*, it's a radical jump, and one step closer to the restructuring of the conventional jazz ensemble that happened on *Bitches Brew* the following year.

The remaining tracks on *Filles de Kilimanjaro* were made earlier in the year, over three days in June and with the old group. Their quality underlines what a challenge it would be for Miles to maintain the same standard with new personnel, though there's a certain irony in the quintet's return to form on the eve of its disbandment. The title piece - and the name can be explained by Miles's investment with actor Jim Brown in a coffee company called Kilimanjaro - reveals how important "Stuff" had been in Miles's creative evolution, but it also shows a more orthodox movement between theme and variations, though intriguingly the original melody dissipates after being strongly stated and restated at the beginning. There is no thematic reprise at the end. "Petits Machins" also sounds like a more remote variant on "Stuff" and indeed has the alternative title "Little Stuff". It's steeped in the blues, though the tonality is implicit rather than actual. It conjures up one of Miles's most brilliant solos, sophistication grounded in the most simple of materials. Its only rival on the album is his feature on the curiously structured "Tout de Suite", which also prompts Shorter's last great tenor solo for Miles.

The piece is unusual in that it sounds as though the opening and closing theme has no formal connection to the main improvised section. This again looks forward to the way in which Teo Macero would juxtapose and splice apparently unrelated tape sections on the later *In a Silent Way* and *Bitches Brew*, giving the music of Miles's electric period its challengingly abstract, constructivist character and collage effects.

On the cover of *Filles de Kilimanjaro* and on the next two albums, Columbia printed the words: "Directions in music by Miles Davis". Miles's development over late 1967 and 1968 not only pointed to a move away from song-based, theme-and-solo improvisation but also in the direction of a new way of recording jazz. For some time, just as there had been a difference in the way Miles was presented on album covers and how he appeared in concert, there was a strong difference in the other direction between the way he played in studio and the much more radical format of his live performances. Increasingly, these were not broken down into separate songs, but had become long, continuous improvisations in which the group moved from one idea to the next, sometimes in accord with enigmatic instructions from the leader, but just as often intuitively. It seemed a logical next step to apply this technique to recording as well.

The idea of the studio as a musical instrument and of the recording engineer and producer as a fellow-musician was becoming standard procedure in pop, but was not new in jazz, either. Charles Mingus's *The Black Saint and the Sinner Lady*, recorded in January 1963, had made full use of splices and overdubs to create a seamless jazz suite, albeit marketed as "The new wave of folk" by Impulse! Records, Mingus was just as ambivalent as Miles about the term jazz. Miles was, in fact, increasingly dismissive of it, not so much because jazz was marginalised by virtue of race but more because budgets for pop recording were already larger and because new marketing philosophies were pushing jazz into a niche, or ghetto.

As so often in his career, fresh thinking about his music often coincided with, and was fuelled by, new creative associations. When in 1985, Miles recorded *Aura*, a magnificent trumpet "concerto" written for him by Danish composer Palle Mikkelborg (see chapter 12) he insisted on sharing the limelight with a musician who for a time 15 years before had been as important an interpreter of his work as John Coltrane, Bill Evans or Wayne Shorter in the past, and another, younger, saxophone-playing Bill Evans in the future. Like Dave Holland, guitarist John McLaughlin was an Englishman who'd grown up playing jazz and rhythm and blues. In the early weeks of 1969, he was in New York, auditioning with Tony Williams's new group Lifetime (which would also feature pianist/organist Larry Young, another class of '69 Miles alumnus). Williams took him to meet Miles, who ordered McLaughlin to show up at Columbia's studios the following day, February 18 1969. Another new recruit got even less notice. Joe Zawinul was telephoned on the morning of the recording session and asked to bring along some scores.

One of those pieces was to mark an epoch in Miles's recording career,

Dave Holland on stage with Miles Davis and Chick Corea at a Jazz Festival in Texas. 1969

in Zawinul's, and in the history of recorded jazz. "In a Silent Way" was originally a complex, multi-chordal conception, very European in tonality. Miles, however, insisted that it be stripped to essentials and played over a single E chord, which gives its quiet, *misterioso* air even more impact. The instrumentation was unprecedented in jazz. McLaughlin played electric guitar with the leader's gnomic instruction - "Play it like you don't know

how to play the guitar" - echoing in his head. Wayne Shorter played
soprano saxophone. This was the instrument Miles had bought for John
Coltrane at the end of their association, and that may have resonated with
him as Shorter began to drift away from the group; whatever the reason
- and it may simply be that he had tired of the "jazz" sound of the alto and
tenor, with their unbreakable connection to Johnny Hodges and Charlie
Parker, Coleman Hawkins, Lester Young and John Coltrane - Miles in

future frequently required his saxophonists to play soprano. Holland and the soon to depart Williams anchored what can no longer accurately be called the rhythm section. Uniquely, though, the group was completed by no less than three electric keyboardists, with Chick Corea and Herbie Hancock on electric pianos, and Joe Zawinul doubling electric piano and organ. There has always been some doubt about the role of different keyboard players on Miles's albums of this period, doubt largely clarified by Paul Tingen's research for his book *Miles Beyond*, but there is no doubt whatsoever about their effect. The music is swirling, ambiguous, richly textured, but with a mournful austerity and with no solo features to give it a point of dramatic focus.

At this point in his career, Miles simply instructed his engineer to leave the tape machines running in order to capture every sound made in the studio. In the editing suite, Miles and Macero cut down the tapes, almost like a sculptor and his assistant chipping away at marble to reveal an essence of form concealed inside. So radical was Miles's editing that not enough was left of "In a Silent Way" to complete an LP side. It was at this point that the decision was taken simply to play parts of the music again, giving the whole performance a hypnotic circularity.

The central episode of side two of the album, bracketed by "In a Silent Way" and its reprise, is a separate piece, "It's About That Time", a flowing, themeless idea closely related to the work on *Filles de Kilimanjaro*. Miles, McLaughlin and Shorter all solo, but with remarkable economy and absolutely in keeping with Miles's initially puzzling instructions, which were intended to avoid "jazz" cliche and to prevent the musicians from relying on conventional dramatic effects or resolutions. Though again the tonality is very static, the players are given remarkable freedom to play whatever they choose.

The first side of the record also consists of a long, continuous piece built over a single chord, and again constructed in the editing room. "Shhh/ Peaceful" is actually more radical and certainly more innovative in terms of Miles's longer term development in that it has no obvious architecture at all, simply a series of musical episodes, all of them cleverly understated, which taken together create almost a landscape effect. (It's no accident that Miles the art-lover and successful graphic artist should evoke analogies from the visual arts: constructivism, collage, sculpture, impressionist landscape.) Unlike the usual linear form of Western music, one feels one could enter or leave "Shhh/Peaceful" at almost any point. To that extent it might almost seem the ancestor of the ambient music of the 1980s and 1990s - and many of those composers have pointed to the Miles of this period as an influence - but for the even stronger feeling that here, almost more than at any other time in his career, Miles is still profoundly rooted in the oldest forms of black American music: the blues, field songs and hollers.

The posthumous *Complete In a Silent Way Sessions* includes an unreleased cut called "The Ghetto Walk", which is suffused with blues feeling. "It's About That Time" is mostly cast in F and also inescapably recalls the blues. There are two trumpet solos, a brief one at the beginning, slightly offhand, and then the main statement after McLaughlin and Shorter have made their contributions. Miles's playing, with its bent notes, tailed-off, asymmetrical phrases and complex air of stoical defiance, raw humour and challenge, is not so far in spirit from the raucous narratives and plaintive songs of loss he must have heard as a child with his grandparents in Arkansas.

The execution and the sound of the group may have been completely new; the concept of bracketing free-form solos with an unrelated introduction and reprise went back not just to the June 1968 sessions for *Filles* but to some of the classic sessions with Gil Evans (notably the flamenco-inspired pieces on *Sketches of Spain*) while the whole feel of the album must have taken even the most startled and sceptical listeners back a full decade. If Ian Carr is correct and Miles's career did move in ten-year cycles, then the music on *In a Silent Way*, with its sketched-in themes, low-key sonority and timeless, antilinear cast, can also be traced back to *Kind of Blue*. It is unquestionably a masterpiece on that scale. Once again, though, Miles was set to shock fans and critics with a another dramatic change of register - and another shift in his visual presentation - that would unsettle expectation and further disguise the deep continuities of an increasingly fractured career.

Extrasensory Perception

Myth and misunderstanding stalked Miles Davis during his life - and have followed him into eternity - but nowhere more unhelpfully than with regard to his music of the early 1970s and after. A casual scan of reference books and jazz histories uncovers a slew of casually unexamined claims: that Miles "invented" jazz-rock; that with *Bitches Brew* he abandoned jazz altogether, not so much turning his back on the past as applying a scorched-earth policy to his art; that he progressively abandoned creative music in favour of a kind of display (what one literary critic in another context called "the performing self"); most ludicrously, that he had somehow fallen out of love with the trumpet as completely as he had fallen out of love with Frances, and with Betty.

In his history of jazz-rock, British historian Stuart Nicholson accords *Bitches Brew* a pivotal place in the development of the genre. Pivotal is exactly the right word. Miles alone did not initiate the genre. By 1968 vibraphonist Gary Burton was experimenting with rock forms. One of his sidemen, guitarist Larry Coryell was exploring ways of assimilating the highly distorted, feedback-laden sound of Jimi Hendrix (who Miles greatly admired) to jazz; Coryell's first wife Julie co-wrote a book, forerunner to Nicholson's, called *Jazz-Rock Fusion,* which included an interview with Miles. Flutist Herbie Mann and saxophonist Charles Lloyd (whose group included Keith Jarrett and Jack DeJohnette) were moving towards a rock sensibility. In Britain, future biographer Ian Carr and his band Nucleus were moving towards what he called in an album title *Elastic Rock.* And it might be argued that the long-form improvisations of bands like the Grateful Dead (who like Miles played rather differently in live performance, swapping folkish songs for extended abstraction) and British supergroup

Cream (essentially a jazz group who also played, blues, R&B and African rhythms) anticipated Miles's slightly later method.

The blending of jazz and rock was in the air. The question was whether the encounter represented a fusion (Julie Coryell's and co-author Laura Friedman's working assumption) or merely an uncomfortable juxtaposition. It's an argument that has continued ever since. In Miles's case, it is relatively easy to resolve. At no time in his career, not even in the pop- and hiphop-flavoured records of the 1980s did he ever entirely abandon a jazz sensibility. Even when the instrumentation, pulse and metre of the music pointed to rock, Miles always played with a strong jazz feel that can't simply be explained by his choice of instrument. Nor did he leave the past behind, but absorbed its lessons into his present thinking. A clear example from 1969 is the piece "Spanish Key", recorded in August for *Bitches Brew*. Both the title and the thirteen-strong ensemble point unmistakably hark back to *Sketches of Spain*. Though Gil Evans wasn't directly involved with the making of *Bitches Brew* and wouldn't collaborate directly with Miles again until the making of *Star People* in 1983, his spirit is still evident in the rich, brooding ensembles. (Significantly, "Star People" itself, metamorphosed into "New Blues", became a staple of Miles's live concerts in the last few years of his life.)

The charge that Miles had lost his appetite for making music, and was becoming content to trade on mere celebrity was a curious inverse outcome of his growing celebrity and, following *In a Silent Way,* renewed appetite for playing and recording. The more relaxed and enthusiastic Miles became the more ready he was to talk to the press. Given that he rarely said anything very specific about his work (indeed, was becoming more gnomic and enigmatic as the years went by), journalists frequently had more to say about Miles the dresser, Miles the boxer, Miles the driver of a bullet-holed red Ferrari, Miles the companion of beautiful women than about Miles the musician. To a degree, their dilemma was a real one. By 1969, Miles had abandoned most of the familiar building blocks of jazz performance - song-forms, vertical harmony, themes and solos - and relied instead on an intuitive approach that was frequently

Miles photographed at home. 1970

mysterious even to his most trusted players and interpreters, who speak of his "telepathic" abilities (Hancock, Holland) or of his "extrasensory perception" (Carr - echoing *E.S.P.*). The main thrust of Paul Tingen's argument in *Miles Beyond* is that the trumpeter was no longer merely a group leader, but some kind of Zen master. During his later interest in the work of Karlheinz Stockhausen, Miles must have identified closely with some elements of the composer's "Intuitive Music". At this stage in his career, he appeared to conduct his ensembles by sheer force of personality, investing glances and gestures with more musical information than might be gleaned from a sheaf of scores or chord structures.

Those who knew Miles best at this period attest to his renewed energy, positive attitude and physical health. In addition to giving up drugs (for the moment), Miles had also renounced all the richly spiced meals - chilis, hashes, spaghetti, fish marinated in Jack Daniel's whisky - which he'd cooked up at the West 77th Street house. His diet was simple, light, almost macrobiotic and there is a corresponding clarity in his trumpet playing of the time. The music of *Bitches Brew* and after might be dark and troublous, but Miles's trumpet sound - admittedly sometimes abetted by amplification - is strong, clear and intense. Just as he took on an almost shamanic presence with his musicians, he invested the trumpet with a mystical significance. Only ill-health in the mid-70s, and not any jadedness or creative dis-satisfaction, forced him to set it aside. By the end of his life, Miles was prepared to undergo acute discomfort, exhaustion and sometimes intense pain in order to continue playing, wearing a rubber corset to maintain his diaphragm, battling with the same slackening cheek-muscle problem that gave Dizzy Gillespie his famous bullfrog look.

His spirits may have been light. The music he made in 1969 was anything but. *Bitches Brew* explores a very different mood and sound-world to *In A Silent Way*. Where the earlier album is quiet, elegiac and expressionistic, with a strong - if unconventional -structure, *Bitches Brew* is turbulent, abstract and open-form. With the arrival of Jack DeJohnette to replace Tony Williams, the rhythmic axis of the group was much more solid. On upright bass, Dave Holland was a more swinging player than electric bassist Harvey Brooks who also took part in the sessions and enjoyed a closer rapport with DeJohnette than with his predecessor. Miles, though, decided to augment the group, adding two percussionists - Jumma Santos and Don Alias - on "Sanctuary", the only Wayne Shorter composition on the album, and more elaborate changes elsewhere.

With Shorter playing soprano only, Miles may have decided the group sound needed more "bottom". With that in mind, he hired multi-instrumentalist Bennie Maupin to play bass clarinet on some of the tracks, and notably the title piece. Maupin was not engaged as a third solo horn; mostly he doubles and elaborates the keyboard shapes, but his rich, chesty sound is a key component on "Bitches Brew" and "Miles Runs the Voodoo Down". For the title track, Miles also added a second electric pianist, Joe Zawinul, who also played on his own "Pharoah's Dance", electric guitarist John McLaughlin, and replaced Holland and DeJohnette with the more rock-oriented Brooks and Lenny White. On "Miles Runs the Voodoo Down", which became the new album's best known cut, Zawinul was replaced by Larry Young, but on "Spanish Key" there are no less than three electric pianos, with Chick Corea, Young and Zawinul all adding to the shimmering, texturally dense backdrop. Later in the year, Miles added two Indian musicians to the group, and between 1970 and 1972 occasionally added tabla, tambura and other subcontinental instruments to the mix.

The result is not so much a big band as a small group with a massively expanded rhythm section. In his autobiography, Miles recalls that his new pool of players - he names 37 - was known in the music business as "Miles Davis's Joint Stock Company". What exact share each had in the creation of his music remains uncertain. There is debate as to who precisely played on the various *Bitches Brew* sessions. Some questions remain about the disposition of keyboard players and discographer Brian Priestley mentions that drummer Billy Cobham, who joined the group in November, believes he was present.

These uncertainties are not simply explained by poor documentation or faulty memory. The nature of the music had changed, and in ways that subordinated all individual contributions to the collective. Joe Zawinul told the author that he found the sessions confusing and unsatisfactory but that later, while visiting Columbia's offices on business relating to his own group Weather Report, he heard an office worker playing a record of intensely powerful music. She was astonished that he did not recognise his own playing on *Bitches Brew.*

The new method subordinated all individual contibutions except one. Miles is in total command throughout. His trumpet sound is fiery and technically superb, though here and there processed with echo, a forerunner to his later use of a wah-wah pedal. The other soloists offer only episodic material. As he does throughout Miles's career, Ian Carr likens the impression to that of a preacher and congregation in the black church, exchanging calls and responses. The difference here is that the preacher, armed with a new, apocalyptic message, does not invoke "Hallelujahs" and "Amens", but an atmosphere of anxiety, even dread. The only exception is the track called "John McLaughlin", on which the guitarist is the only featured soloist, with Miles and Shorter both sitting out.

Another source of uncertainty is the method by which the album was put together. Much has been said about producer Teo Macero's role, sometimes to the extent that he is claimed as co-composer. The reality is that Miles and Macero began the sessions on unusually poor terms, an atmosphere which might explain the ferocity of the trumpet playing, and Macero did his usual production and editing job, but far less pro-actively than on *In A Silent Way* or the later *Jack Johnson.* Because there were no pre-determined songs, structures or even chord progressions, the musicians did not know what they were playing; they were simply playing, with Miles controlling the process more by gesture than through specifically musical instructions.

Bitches Brew is a long album, containing more than an hour and a half of music. It was released as a double LP, with a surreally beautiful gatefold sleeve. The artist Mati Klarwein (later Abdul Mati) was a former student of Fernand Leger and friend of Salvador Dali. He grew up in Palestine, the son of refugees from Nazi Germany, and his work often evokes exile and journeying. Klarwein also painted the cover art for Miles's *Live-Evil*, where he deliberately juxtaposes beauty - a pregnant African woman whose cicatrised belly is being kissed by a spirit - with grotesque ugliness. *Bitches Brew* is a less confusing document than the 1972 album and the art-work reflects its beautifully balanced mix of physicality and yearning spirituality.

That mood is established from Miles's first entry on "Pharoah's Dance", the first track. He plays tentative phrases, hinting at a complex tonality, or no clear tonality at all. Soprano and bass clarinet pose questions. Miles responds more ringingly and with a cavernous echo. The whole track might be a Socratic dialogue or, given the title, some Egyptian ritual of the dead - Maupin's bass clarinet evoking an underworld presence, Shorter wheeling overhead like a kestrel, Miles as burnished as the sun.

It's the only track that points to a definite continuity with *In a Silent Way*. The remainder of the album points elsewhere, both back and forward. "Spanish Key" has a strong rock beat, but the harmonic language is irresistibly reminiscent of the collaborations with Gil Evans. Miles's trumpet playing, though, is far more muscular and assertive than on the earlier record, still tinged with sadness but with a new defiance. "Bitches Brew" is likewise reminiscent of his work with Evans, but the faintly classical, *concertante* mode has been replaced by a far robuster dialogue and a more evenly balanced rate of exchange between soloist and ensemble. The impression is almost of a tiny David defying the giant and gaining in stature almost as we listen. The echo effects lend his top notes an additional presence, making this one of the most powerful performances of his whole career, purely in terms of trumpet playing. "Miles Runs the Voodoo Down" was the track chosen for airplay and for jukeboxes. It's a simple enough conception, deeply rooted in the blues, and with a clearer logic and line than most of the rest of *Bitches Brew*. Again, the trumpet playing is remarkable and serves to confound the often-repeated assertion that Miles avoided the upper register and strong dynamics. As with the other long tracks, there are internal divisions that give the piece much drama. Miles's first solo is incendiary. Wayne Shorter responds in kind,

Bitches Brew cover art by Mati Klarwein

with Maupin circling him like a sparring partner. Miles re-enters and then unexpectedly drives the ensemble in a new rhythmic direction which he controls through further changes of mood until the track winds down.

If *Bitches Brew* marked an epoch in Miles's career, the reasons were not entirely musical. The cover art was directed at a rock audience, an impression retrospectively confirmed when Klarwein went on to create a sleeve image for Santana's *Abraxas* and other rock records. This was also the time when Miles and his group finally shrugged off formal stage attire in favour of brightly coloured casual clothes. Suits and ties would certainly have looked out of place at the Fillmore East. Promoter Bill Graham's New York hall was *the* rock venue of the time. Its twin was in San Francisco, and Miles and his group appeared at both several times during 1970.

This was a period of intense activity for him, playing and recording most days, and looking around for a replacement for Wayne Shorter, who was departing to co-found Weather Report. For a time, Miles shrewdly overlapped Shorter with the teenage Steve Grossman - ostensibly hired to replace Bennie Maupin as second reed on the February 27date which is part of the background to the *Jack Johnson* sessions - but by the time the new sextet (with percussionist Airto Moreira) played the Fillmore West on April 10, Grossman was established as soprano saxophonist. The pattern of recruiting very young musicians was to continue through Miles's career. The logic was simple. Miles only recruited the most proficient players, but at 18 or 19 or 20 there was little risk that they had settled into a personal style and less risk that they would quickly leave such a prestigious gig and move on to their own careers.

Shorter was still on hand when Miles made his debut at the Fillmore East on March 6 and 7 1970 on a bill that included the Steve Miller Band and Neil Young and Crazy Horse. The music from the second night was subsequently issued on disc and confirms the story that Miles refused to compromise in any way to a rock audience. His and the group's playing is ruggedly and for many of those who attended, mystifyingly abstract. The much bootlegged recording wasn't officially released until 2001, but

Miles's later engagements for Graham were issued at the time as *Black Beauty* (Fillmore West, April 10) and *Live at Fillmore* (East, June 17 - 20), the latter an absurdly edited collage of muddled segues and repeated themes. In August, Miles appeared on the same bill as Jimi Hendrix at the Isle of Wight rock festival in England, a performance which is also available on disc and video.

By then, though, he had completed one of his most remarkable projects - comparable in its influence on his future course to *L'ascenseur pour l'echafaud* - and had also made some of the recordings that would make up the dark, disturbing *Live-Evil.*

In early 1970, Miles had been asked to write music for a documentary film on the boxer Jack Johnson, the first black heavyweight champion of the world and a man who resisted prejudice and lived with a flamboyance that was very much after Miles's own heart. What might to some artists have been a lucrative commercial recording, executed professionally but perfunctorily, was highly personal to Miles, who underlined its importance by writing a sleeve note for the album. The issued version consists of just two long performances, "Right Off" and "Yesternow", but the release of the *Complete Jack Johnson Sessions* in 2004 restored the background to yet another of Miles's creative evolutions.

This time, the catalyst was the increasing unavailability and imminent departure of Dave Holland and the recruitment of another teenager, 19 year old bass guitarist Michael Henderson, who had previously worked with Stevie Wonder and who joined the Miles Davis group full-time towards the end of 1970. At the most obvious level, Henderson seemed a strange choice. Where Holland had been swinging, harmonically subtle and melodically inventive, Henderson preferred to create and sustain a single unchanging groove, often over a single chord or rocking back and forth between two chords. This was precisely what Miles wanted in 1970. For all his eclectic listening in classical music and subsequent enthusiasm for Karlheinz Stockhausen, Miles was concerned that jazz was becoming too formal and losing its roots in folklore. The change in his music with and after *Jack Johnson* is testimony to that.

Black All Right

"I'm black. They never let me forget it. I'm black all right. I'll never let *them* forget it." The words are Jack Johnson's recited by actor Brock Peters right at the end of the record, but the defiant sentiment might just as well be Miles Davis's. Though he had grown up in a middle-class community, Miles had not been immune to racial abuse. One early memory was of being chased down an East St Louis street by a white man who shouted "Nigger! Nigger!" after him. In his dealings with record companies and promoters, Miles always sought to be treated the same - which in practical terms meant better - than white fellow-musicians.

How "black" was his music? It is a fundamental misconception to think that when Miles began to play rock venues he was courting a new white audience. If anything, the opposite was the case. One of the abiding ironies of jazz history is that a music created by African-Americans was largely patronised by well-off whites. The changes in Miles's music after 1970, were if anything an attempt to re-align himself with a black constituency, the kind of imaginary community evoked in Corky Hale's cover art for 1972's *On the Corner*. Miles's realignment was similar to that of his young friend Prince who in the 1980s largely abandoned the tough, "Uptown" sensibility of early albums like *Dirty Mind* in favour of the funk-pop crossover that brought him massive success with *Purple Rain*, but then turned away from white pop and repositioned his music quite self-consciously in a black continuum.

Miles and Prince were to enjoy a warm, but ultimately somewhat unproductive relationship. It seemed set to fulfil the thwarted promise of his creative friendship with Jimi Hendrix. Despite apparently losing Betty to him, Miles was close to and admired the guitarist, presumably also envying him the enormous crowds he was capable of drawing. There were plans afoot for Hendrix to record with Miles and Gil Evans when he died suddenly in London. Hendrix's funeral was a major trauma from which some say Miles never entirely recovered. There were other pressures in Miles's life. Though he and new girlfriend Marguerite Eskridge had a new son, and though he became a grandfather at the same time, thanks to his daughter Cheryl, Miles's other children were causing him anxiety and disappointment. Cheryl's young brother Gregory, like his father a second child with a shrewd supportive older sister, came back from Vietnam alienated and depressed, infuriated Miles by adopting a Black Muslim name, while Miles IV, anxious at 20 to get out from under his father's name and shadow, also rebelled. However proud he was of Cheryl, she had returned to teach school in St Louis and kept her distance from the music business; by her own account, she was over 50 before she set foot in a recording studio. It was another of those periods in Miles's life where people seemed to be abandoning him at a moment of creative turbulence.

The music on *Jack Johnson* exactly fits that description. It also reflected how idiosyncratically Miles now approached the recording process. Had Cheryl been present at the Columbia studios on April 7 1970, she would have seen nothing happening for many long minutes, while her father talked to Teo Macero in the control booth. Gradually, John McLaughlin, bassist Michael Henderson and drummer Billy Cobham began to play a boogie figure, the kind of thing musicians do to keep their playing "muscles" flexible prior to a recording. Suddenly the red light came on and Miles rushed into the studio and started playing.

"Right Off" was thus created spontaneously. The other music on *Jack Johnson* was, however, subject to considerable editing. In addition to Peters' narration, "Yesternow" includes an element recorded earlier in the year (February 18) with guitarist Sonny Sharrock and Jack DeJohnette, an edit from "Shhh/Peaceful" on *In A Silent Way* and other materials arranged by Macero and released on his own imprint as a separate album. The *Complete Jack Johnson Sessions* also reveals tracks like "Go Ahead John" (another namecheck for McLaughlin), "Willie Nelson" and "Duran" (named after

Miles's favourite middleweight boxer) which reveal the same unstructured and spontaneous approach. On "Right Off", Herbie Hancock's organ playing is the other key element, though it is difficult to tell exactly what he is playing, other than weighty aural shapes. This again anticipates the huge keyboard clusters Miles himself explored on electronic keyboards later in the 1970s. Miles's trumpet solo on "Yesternow" is in complete contrast to the brash intensity of the first side. It's a stark and melancholy conception, with the leader's mournful soliloquy again pointed up by fine playing from both McLaughlin and Steve Grossman.

Miles had never before been so productive. The first half of 1970 saw him in the studio no less than fourteen times, accumulating material that in some cases would not be released for some years (as in the case of *Big Fun* and *Get Up With It*), and in others remains unissued in Columbia's vaults. It was the busiest year of his life. In addition to the spring Fillmore concerts, his groups played engagements in Ann Arbor and Philadelphia, and at clubs in San Francisco and Washington, D.C. Recordings made on a return visit to the last of these, the Cellar Door, D.C. in December 1970, went toward the making of one of his most complex and troublings discs. There is nothing else in his official output quite like *Live-Evil*. Not even the notorious live discs *Dark Magus* and *Pangaea*, taken from concerts at Carnegie Hall and the Festival Hall in Osaka, Japan, just before his five-year withdrawal from active playing in 1975, match it for ferocity and darkness of vision.

It is a record that has divided his critics, not least because Miles's trumpet sound, often characterised (misleadingly) as limpid, fragile, elegiac, has taken on a violent and apparently uncontrolled quality, Dionysiac and disordered, heavily processed with amplification and wah-wah. The group sound, too, is radically removed from the blue-toned, almost twilit abstraction that characterised much of his music from *Kind of Blue* to *In a Silent Way*. It also disconcertingly speaks a very different musical language even from the vibrant collage of *Bitches Brew* and the rock-funk grooves of *Jack Johnson*. There are signs that Miles was self-consciously exploring another, darker side of his musical nature, playing to the "Prince of

On a concert tour Miles passes through Heathrow. 1973

115

Darkness" tag that had attached itself to him. The palindromic title is also echoed in the (ironically Muslim-sounding) name "Selim Sivad" which serves as *alter ego* and separately as the title of two pieces on *Live-Evil*.

It became axiomatic in the 1980s, and even at a point where Miles's evolution had slowed to the point where he was prepared to repeat some solo material night after night, that in order to understand and appreciate his current thinking it was necessary not just to buy the studio recordings but also to attend concerts or amass a shelf-full of bootleg tapes. That was much more obvious in 1970. Having been suspicious of live recording before the Blackhawk albums, Miles, Macero and Columbia seemed almost addicted to it. Unusually, though it was also the pattern of Weather Report's *I Sing the Body Electric* (issued in 1972), *Live-Evil* is a mixture of club and studio tapes. The earliest track is "Double Image", recorded in February with Shorter, Corea, Zawinul (playing his own composition), McLaughlin, Holland, DeJohnette, Cobham and Moreira. In June, Miles brought back Hancock, and added the remarkable Brazilian multi-instrumentalist Hermeto Pascoal and add three more tracks, though "Selim" and "Nem Um Talvez" are actually versions of the same Pascoal composition.

At the end of the year, Miles again called on McLaughlin to join the group at the Cellar Door, a decision which some observers (and some of the musicians) thought unbalanced the group, but which contributed greatly to the boiling intensity of the club material on *Live-Evil*. "What I Say" is almost unbearably intense, though in the opinion of the record's detractors it sacrifices subtlety for power, an observation Miles would probably have taken as a positive comment rather than a negative criticism. Holland had played at the Isle of Wight appearance months earlier before leaving the group to join Corea in a short-lived avant-group called Circle. Now, though, Michael Henderson was confirmed as a full-time member, contributing his clever and only deceptively crude bass figures to a piece in which the rhythm section does no more than create a hard, motoric groove for the soloists. Keith Jarrett demonstrates his brilliance and new saxophonist Gary Bartz's raw sound suited Miles's new music better than Shorter's would have done. Bartz plays an intense soprano solo, doubling briefly on flute, an instrument that began to figure in Miles's groups for the first time around this period.

Jarrett also plays superbly on "Funky Tonk", which some discographies split into several titles, including "Inamorata", a curious item with an overdubbed narration by actor Conrad Roberts. "Sivad" is more stately, but the atmosphere and the leader's trumpet playing are in a new dramatic vein which most observers have been tempted to declare unprecedented in the history of jazz. Paul Tingen seems to regard the music on *Live-Evil* as the product of some heightened state of consciousness. With characteristic acuity, Ian Carr likens it to "some of Duke Ellington's jungle music". Given Miles's later tributes to one of jazz's great composers, such as "He Loved Him Madly", recorded in 1974, this is also prescient. In 1970, the ageing Ellington was virtually an establishment figure, venerated and feted even by the musical mainstream, composing and presenting a series of "Sacred Concerts". What Miles admired was the fierce, anarchic music of earlier years, when Ellington had cleverly subverted white audiences' expectation of black musicians with compositions like "Jungle Blues", "Jungle Nights in Harlem" and similar. Miles must also have had a certain affection for "East St Louis Toodle-oo", if only for nostalgic reasons. His later attempt, in one observer's vivid phrase, to marry the sound-worlds of Duke Ellington and Karlheinz Stockhausen was further evidence of his careful blend of avant-garde experiment and a deep understanding of the whole jazz tradition.

Whether the music on *Live-Evil* is "jazz" or not is an open and in some respects a redundant question. It does not swing in the conventional sense; it involves little in the way of song-form and less in the way of harmonic progression; and yet its atmosphere and spirit belong unmistakably to an African-American continuum whose most adventurous expression was in jazz. Whether such a view still applied to Miles's next studio record, or indeed to much of the work he made between the end of 1970 and his death in 1991 is more of a moot question.

"It was with *On The Corner* and *Big Fun* that I really made an effort to get my music over to young black people. . . . I had started thinking about building an audience for the future." In musical terms, the

Miles in performance. c1970

building materials could hardly have seemed more varied. As he goes on the explain in his autobiography, "It was actually a combination of some of the concepts of Paul Buckmaster, Sly Stone, James Brown and Stockhausen, [and] some of the concepts I had absorbed from Ornette [Coleman]'s music, [what he] had said about things being played three or four ways, independently of each other". Ever the voracious listener, Miles had been introduced to Karlheinz Stockhausen's music, by Paul Buckmaster, a young English cellist and composer he had met in London. Typically, though, Miles wanted to wed the shimmering electronic sound-world of Stockhausen's "Telemusik" to the raw, ambiguous harmonics and multiple rhythms of what Coleman later referred to as "harmolodics". Dismissed as a charlatan as often as he is hailed as a visionary, Coleman was one of the few jazz avant-gardists for whom Miles reserved a measure of respect. Even greater, though, was his enthusiasm for the funky energy of Sly Stone, an untrained musician who like Miles himself took ideas from his band and melded them into songs like "Dance to the Music" and "Stand". Miles claimed to have worn out his copies of both.

In citing these new enthusiasms, he was, however, insistent that as ever he was his own model, and not dependent on anyone else's system. To some degree, learning about Stockhausen can only have confirmed his own intuitive method. Buckmaster says, "I related to Miles some of the thoughts and ideas of Stockhausen, like 'play something next to what you hear' and 'think of what comes before what you're playing and what comes after it'". Listeners searching for a "Stockhausen influence" on Miles's music of the early 1970s are fated to be misled or else to wonder whether the comment in that notoriously inconsistent and mischievous autobiography really was in earnest.

Insofar as it is possible to trace the impact of other musics on the work recorded after *Bitches Brew*, such "influences" have to be heard in a generalised philosophical sense and only in keeping with Miles's desire to create a music that was increasingly folkloric and immediate rather than abstract and generic. The release history of the sessions recorded between November 1969 and October 1974, shortly before Miles's five year retirement from active music-making, is complex: *Get Up With It* was a blend of second-rank material from 1972 (including "Rated X", one of Miles's first recorded forays on electric organ), "Red China Blues" from an uneasy January 1973 studio date, and three magnificent tracks from late May and June 1974. These include "He Loved Him Madly", a deeply felt and haunting electronic threnody to another great influence, Duke Ellington, who died on May 24; here, at least, the Stockhausen influence is palpable, but not elsewhere. *Big Fun* was less to Miles's liking since most of the music on it was half a decade old. The exception was "Ife", which unusually he continued to play even after his comeback in the early 1980s. It was a left-over from the controversial *On The Corner* sessions.

Buckmaster was summoned to New York in the late spring of 1972 and spent several weeks with Miles, listening to classical records and discussing the methods and philosophy of Indian music. It was a friendship that continued for some years, but on June 1, Buckmaster found himself cast in a similar role to Gil Evans, acting as midwife to an inchoate body of material and a sprawling, eclectic ensemble who far from having formal scores or charts to read were expected to work largely by instinct. Fortunately, some members - Chick Corea, Herbie Hancock, John McLaughlin, Bennie Maupin and Jack DeJohnette - were already familiar with Miles's methods. Bassist Mike Henderson approached his role with youthful self-confidence. New drummer Billy Hart was shortly to be replaced by the brilliant Al Foster, who remained one of Miles's most loyal friends and interpreters, even when he sometimes doubted the validity of the music. Don Alias and Mtume (actually James Heath jr, son of saxophonist Jimmy Heath and member of a prodigiously gifted musical family) were the percussionists. At this period, the soprano saxophonist role rotated between Sonny Fortune, Carlos Garnett and the technically and intellectually formidable Dave Liebman, who had succeeded Steve Grossman and Gary Bartz. Liebman quickly recognized that his role in the group was not that of a featured soloist, but despite the leader's belittling comments he remained intensely loyal to Miles and, like Foster, contributed generously to his creative rehabilitation in 1982. The other members of the group were electric sitarist Collin Walcott (later of the group Oregon) and keyboard player Harold Williams, who was simply around the studio with friends.

The analogy between Buckmaster and Evans evaporates on first hearing *On The Corner*. The first, disconcerting aural impression is that Miles Davis isn't playing on his own record. Where Evans had him front and forward in the mix, as clear and dominant as a concerto soloist, here Miles is often buried away in the ensemble, his heavily wah-wahed trumpet sounding more like an electric guitar than the clarion of "Saeta". Though "Black Satin", the short second track, restores something of his trumpet lyricism, but mostly the music is thickly collective, with origins in African and Asian music rather than Western forms. Here, and in the band that played at Philharmonic Hall in September 1972 (a performance recorded and released by Columbia), Miles used electric sitar as a way of creating drones and the tabla as a way of setting up different patterns of rhythm to the 4/4 and 6/8 metres of conventional jazz. Michael Henderson's deliberately pared down bass lines, often just two alternated notes, create a groove of hypnotic presence.

"Black Satin" may have been a small backward glance. The twenty-minute "suite" that opens *On the Corner* most certainly is not. McLaughlin's highly distorted guitar and Liebman's controlled but piercing soprano lines are distinguishable, but the presence of five percussionists and the drones and ostinati set up by the remaining stringed instruments gives the piece - made up of "On the Corner", "New York Girl", "Thinkin' One Thing and Doin' Another" and "Vot" - give it a surging ambiguity that defeats all anticipation of conventional development (it's even difficult to tell where one piece segues into another) and helps explain why Miles refused to put the musicians' names on the cover.

What he had instead was another painting, this time by Corky Hale rather than Klarwein and effectively a caricature of the Harlem street types: latter-day zoot-suiters, huge Afros and shades, steatopygous women, gays and a couple of token whites. It's a not entirely clear representation

Cicely Tyson photographed at a reception in London. 1973

of the music within, though it does make clear Miles's ambition to be seen as a street-wise brother rather than a button-collared "jazz" musician. Unfortunately, Columbia still saw Miles's music in that demographic and the record was only pushed to jazz stations, not the rock and R&B stations that young blacks in America listened to. Though the record sold respectably, some 50,000 copies on release, it wasn't the crossover success

Miles had anticipated. His fury was compounded when a year later his former pianist Herbie Hancock released a funk record called *Headhunters* (subsequently also the name of his group) and it became a million-seller, perversely dubbed the biggest selling jazz album of all time.

In September 1972, shortly before release, Miles developed some aspects of his *On the Corner* music at Philharmonic Hall in New York, with saxophonist Carlos Garnett, keyboard player Cedric Lawson, guitarist Reggie Lucas, electric sitarist Khalil Balakrishna, and Henderson, Foster, Mtume and Badal Roy. The event was recorded and issued with a yet more colourful Corky Hale cover as *In Concert*, a curiously formal title for such funky music, delivered in four untitled slabs. There is an irony in that Lincoln Center, where Philharmonic Hall is located, had for the previous thirteen years also been the home of Miles's uneasy *alma mater*, the Juilliard School.

Unfortunately he was not able to prop up sales of the new album with the usual tour. Less than two weeks after Philharmonic Hall, Miles crashed his sports car in Manhattan, broke both legs and cut his face. The injuries put him out of action until June of the following year. They also compounded existing health and personal problems. Miles had pulmonary problems and suffered from gallstones. He had split up with Betty Davis in 1969. Subsequent affairs with Marguerite Eskridge (who is pictured on the cover of *At Fillmore*) and Jackie Battle, a 20 year old secretary at the United Nations, were no less stormy. Eskridge was in Miles's car when he was shot at by drug dealers. Battle reacted to her lover's apparently runaway cocaine use by taking sleeping tablets; when Miles went out on crutches to buy his drug of choice, she ended the relationship. An affair with Sherry 'Peaches' Brewer followed but it wasn't until Cicely Tyson came back into his life that Miles achieved a measure of personal tranquility.

By then, Miles had been locked in a physical and creative trough for more than two years, only leaving his increasingly dirty and shabby house to buy drugs, seeing few of his old friends and showing little interest in making music. Like his father, he had been shrewd in his investments and his records had all paid off their advances, so money, which has driven many jazz musicians to keep working in a physical state even worse than Miles Davis's, was not for the moment an issue. Appetite for performance was. Live appearances in the early 70s became excruciatingly mannered, Miles's stage persona caught somewhere between arrogant contempt for his audience and a self-importance that was all the more poignant as it became clear he was a desperately sick man. Miles's hip problems had recurred and he was unable to take the exercise that seemed to lift him out of depression and energise his playing. He suffered pneumonia in 1975 having returned from a Far East tour and having played the Newport Festival for the last time. Only in December of that year was he strong enough for the hip-replacement surgery needed to keep him ambulatory. In 1978, he served a further short prison term for failing to pay maintenance to Marguerite Eskridge for their son. His personal decline seemed complete.

Columbia had a substantial body of recording in the vaults and were sufficiently respectful of Miles's artistic importance to put him on a special retainer, but his last two records before his retirement were only deemed suitable for release in Japan where they had been recorded in concert. The music on *Agharta* and *Pangaea* is dark, roiling and muddled, with few reference points from the past, though "Theme from Jack Johnson" does figure. Though there is some fine playing from a powerful rhythm section, from the two guitarists Pete Cosey and Reggie Lucas and from saxophonist Sonny Fortune, Miles himself sounds unfocused and cut off, frequently content to stab out dense organ clusters rather than play trumpet. The posthumously released *Dark Magus* documents a slightly earlier concert at Carnegie Hall, with Azar Lawrence joining Dave Liebman as second saxophonist, and a third electric guitarist added in the shape of Hendrix disciple Dominique Gaumont. While the guitarists vie with one another for attention, Miles simply sounds lost, in perplexing and heartbreaking contrast to his appearance in the same hall in may 1961. In searching for a new audience, he appeared to have lost one that had followed him loyally since his emergence with Charlie Parker two decades earlier. There had been periods of creative uncertainty and confusion before. This time, though, Miles's decline seemed irreversible.

Time After Time

In early June 1981, Miles Davis made a tentative return to live performance, a ten minute guest spot with members of the Mel Lewis band at a New York club. He played a blues. There was a poignant irony in the moment, not just because it anticipated a last decade much given over to cameo roles, but also because Lewis's big band partner, trumpeter and composer Thad Jones, a man Miles greatly admired, had walked out of one of his 1970s concerts in bafflement and disgust at the direction Miles had taken. Three weeks after that cautious re-emergence, Miles Davis and a new group played four nights at a small (capacity less than 500) club in Boston called Kix. Just over a week later, he returned to a scene of past glories when he played two concerts at Avery Fisher Hall, formerly Philharmonic Hall, as part of the Kool Jazz Festival, the successor to the Newport Festival.

The changed names were only another sign of how much had changed since he had been away. The 1970s had been difficult times for jazz, with fusion groups dominating the scene and few major musicians resistant to the lure of a watered-down version of the eclectic, electric approach Miles had helped to pioneer. While he languished, former band members became major stars - Chick Corea, John McLaughlin, Joe Zawinul and Wayne Shorter in Weather Report, Herbie Hancock above all - and he became more and more a figure from the past. A new and in a different way controversial trumpet star was waiting in the wings. In 1981, Wynton Marsalis recorded his debut album for Miles's own label and using some of the the men - Ron Carter, Tony Williams - who had helped shape his musical vision a generation before.

It is often implied - or flatly stated - that Miles took no active interest in music during his period of withdrawal. The truth is that he remained in contact with a few close musician friends, with McLaughlin, Jack and Lydia DeJohnette, and with Al Foster, all of whom helped keep him abreast of new developments. A warm and lasting relationship developed with nephew Vince Wilburn jr, his sister Dorothy's son and a promising percussionist; Vince later became a member of Miles's group, a role which evolved into personal assistant, but more importantly he brokered the tentative sessions which saw Miles return to active playing in 1981. Though two years before, in February 1978, Miles had joined Al Foster and guitarist Larry Coryell in a New York studio, he was too frail and out of practice to play trumpet. British scholar George Cole suggests that more than once Miles talked about putting a band together, but these initiatives came to nothing; he even failed to turn up for one projected session that would have involved his future collaborator, bassist Marcus Miller. The reality is that for the entire span of the extended Columbia contract that ran between 1976 and 1979, he made no releasable music.

The turning point came in 1979. At the most basic level, Miles was running out of money, having spent freely on alcohol, cocaine and other drugs. Columbia were running out of patience, but were still content to play a long game. That year saw the release of a double LP of Miles material, *Circle in the Round*. The title piece was recorded in 1967 and is little more than a slabby, unedited studio jam, of interest to collectors only in that it includes an appearance by another British guitarist, Jeff Beck. "Splash" from the following year was the most recent item in a set that went all the way back to the first great quintet in 1958 ("Love For Sale") and some material from the Blackhawk sessions. Disappointing as it must have been for Miles fans, it was at least a sign that there was still an interest in his work. During that year a New York FM radio station played all of Miles's records, complete and in chronological order, which took almost a week. It would have been a nostalgic experience for old fans and a rapid catch-up exercise for younger listeners.

Cicely Tyson's return to his life held out some hope of a recovery, but there were two other influential friends on the scene. Miles listened to some of the WKCR broadcasts in the company of Paul Buckmaster, who'd

Miles and saxophonist Bill Evans performing in Paris. 1982

Miles Davis in concert. 1987

been called over again to work on some tentative ideas; this led to the abortive session with Miller. At the same time, Columbia vice-president Dr George Butler had begun visiting Miles regularly, gauging his physical and mental health, talking to his company's errant star about every subject except music, but gradually building up the trust that would characterise their working relationship after Miles's comeback.

When Miles did begin to play again, Columbia were so uncertain about his staying power and will to continue that they recorded any live commitments he was able to honour. In an echo of what had happened just before his retirement, the whole of an October 1981 Tokyo event was released in Japan only as *Miles! Miles! Miles!* One song, named after Frances Taylor's son Jean-Pierre, was included with some of the Kix and Avery Fisher Hall material and released as *We Want Miles*.

It wasn't the first album of his comeback. Opinions vary sharply about the quality of music in Miles's final period, but there is a general consensus that the first and last of the comeback records were the weakest of his career. *The Man With the Horn* was largely made with a young Chicago group put together with the help of Vince Wilburn, who was also the band's drummer. Miles made his first studio appearance as a trumpeter for some five years on May 1 1980.

A more lasting association was to follow when Miles started to build a long-term touring band. On the advice of Dave Liebman, Miles recruited a new saxophonist. There was a poignancy to the choice because Bill Evans shared his name with the pianist from the *Kind of Blue* group and *that* Bill Evans had died prematurely in September 1980, worn out by drug abuse. The new Bill Evans became a trusted aide, fulfilling the same role Wilburn would take on later. He also brought a bright contemporary saxophone sound to the group. Miles also experimented with guitar players, before replacing Barry Finnerty with Mike Stern, a powerful rock-influenced player whose own problems with drugs and alcohol meant that his career with the Miles Davis group was intermittent. The electric bassist was Marcus Miller and the drummer was Al Foster. Sometimes a percussionist was added, but this was the core of Miles's comeback group.

"Jean-Pierre" became one of the signature pieces of Miles's later period, along with Cyndi Lauper's "Time After Time" somewhat later. It's a significant piece on a number of levels. In the first place, it is deeply if implicitly rooted in the blues. Secondly, there is some doubt as to its precise authorship. One story suggests that the nursery rhyme-like theme was actually Jean-Pierre's own creation, or possibly something Miles had created to amuse the child. Other versions suggest that Gil Evans (who was again part of Miles's circle) reminded him of a little tag he used to play in solos and the tune developed from there. Either way, it seems to have been in Miles's head for some time and its genesis suggests again how often his most distinctive work was the result of collaborative effort. The other significant thing about these and later performances of "Jean-Pierre" (which appears in two versions on *We Want Miles* and is also part of a medley on 1985's *You're Under Arrest*) is that apart from stating the theme Miles plays very little, leaving the solo space to his band members. This was to be a familiar pattern over his final decade. Miles may have been back in circulation, but his "lip" was suspect, he had ongoing pulmonary problems, and needed a rubber corset to allow him to maintain the air pressure required for trumpet playing. Backstage he was receiving oxygen and frequently needed to be supported physically. If he was understandably not playing at full stretch in 1981, the performance roster of his final years began to resemble some grand tragic processional by an ailing potentate.

Those who had been shocked by his appearance on his comeback - gaunt, frail, visibly ill, a stocking cap pulled down over his thinning hair, later to be replaced by an extravagant wig (see cover photo) - came to concerts as much to observe a pain-wracked spectacle as to listen to music. Like novelist William Burroughs, who spent his last years making guest appearances on rock tours and videos, Miles became a master of the cameo, playing short guest spots on rock albums, writing soundtrack music for movies and appearing on screen in one of them (the Australian-made *Dingo*, playing jazz trumpeter "Billy Cross") and in the television series *Miami Vice* (less obviously typecast, albeit with some personal resonance, as a pimp).

And yet, for all the patchiness of his output and apparent triviality of some of the contexts he chose, for all the obvious health problems and technical shortcomings, for all the sometimes preposterous posturing, Miles still had the ability to move audiences. He could lend a relatively lightweight pop song like Scritti Politi's "Oh Patti (Don't Feel Sorry For Lover Boy)" or Toto's "Don't Stop Me Now" a momentary majesty, or take a theme like Cyndi Lauper's "Time After Time" and Jeff Porcaro's "Human Nature" (made famous by Michael Jackson) and invest it with real jazz feeling. The overlooked story of Miles's final decade is his renewed love affair with jazz and the blues. It's no coincidence in that context that *We Want Miles* should have included a long, heartfelt version of Gershwin's "My Man's Gone Now", the slow lament from *Porgy & Bess*. That Miles should have returned to a tune he first played with Gil Evans more than two decades ago gave the lie to the often-repeated claim that he never looked back and never repeated himself. Having included "Back Street Betty" on *The Man With the Horn*, he broke his usual habit by programming it again, a live edit from Avery Fisher Hall, on *We Want Miles*. Admittedly, the only tunes from his back catalogue he repeated regularly were "Ife", Zawinul's "In A Silent Way" and the Gershwin song, but there were signs that Miles was prepared to revisit his own history on occasion, and twice in the last year of his life - special occasions, both - he reunited with former associates. A regular at Claude Nobs's Montreux Jazz Festival, in July 1991 he agreed to play a set of Gil Evans arrangements with orchestra and big band, conducted by Quincy Jones. Two day later, on July 10, he took part in a remarkable gathering at La Halle, La Villette, Paris, with Chick Corea, Herbie Hancock, Dave Holland, John McLaughlin, saxophonist Jackie McLean (who'd played with Miles on the 1955 *Quintet/Sextet* date for Prestige), and John Scofield. Though Miles's current group was ostensibly the main focus, the reunion with so many musicians who'd been close to him in halcyon days - the event was billed "Miles Davis and Friends" - guaranteed a nostalgic reaction. Just weeks later, Miles Davis was dead. Unexpected as his final decline was, it seemed as if Miles had sensed time was running out and was anxious to tie up loose ends.

The final ten years of Miles Davis's life yielded a further seven studio albums, plus the unreleased *Rubberband* and soundtrack albums from *Siesta* and *Dingo*. Of these, two are masterpieces, though it's possible to argue that the brooding *Tutu* is really a Marcus Miller record with Miles overdubs. The other work of real stature also owes much to a collaborator. *Aura*, recorded after Miles's acceptance of the Sonning Music Award in Denmark in 1984, is an elaborate trumpet concerto written by fellow-trumpeter and Miles disciple Palle Mikkelborg.

The award itself was a unique honour, having previously only been offered to senior classical figures like Stravinsky, Shostakovitch and Leonard Bernstein. Miles was originally only expected to play on the final section of "Aura", as part of the Sonning celebrations, but was so impressed with the Dane's Messiaen-influenced composition, which used a colour code for each section and a tone-row derived from the letters of Miles's name, that it was agreed he should play on a new version. It was recorded in Copenhagen in late January and February 1985 with additional solo parts and features by percussionist Marilyn Mazur, bassists Niels-Henning Ørsted Pedersen and Bo Stief, keyboardplayer Thomas Clausen and with John McLaughlin strongly featured on "White", "Orange" and "Violet". The first of these was not originally part of the suite, but Miles's forceful playing on muted horn makes it one of the early highlights, a spare, uncluttered piece that reflects both Miles's instinctive minimalism and Mikkelborg's interest in classical idioms. "Orange" was a series of leitmotifs intended to conjure up previous distinguished Sonning winners. There are two versions of "Red", the original played on open horn and "Electric Red" with the Harmon mute. One might have expected "Blue" to reflect Miles's *Kind of Blue* period, but it opens on an intriguingly irregular poppy rhythm and only becomes ballad-like two-thirds of the way through when Miles switches again to muted horn. His main reference to the blues comes on the closing "Violet" where again the trumpet switches personalities in the most dramatic way, alternating a gently elegiac feel with some fiery playing.

Miles doesn't play on every track on *Aura* but the finished album, and the slightly augmented reissue, are definitive Miles Davis performances.

Miles displayed an increasingly eccentric taste in clothing on stage

Miles was top billing for the Montreux Jazz Festival of 1986

Mikkelborg's use of subtle synthesizer lines, glockenspiel and other percussion chimes remarkably well with Miles's enthusiasm for drum machines and the record has a unique and wholly consistent sound, only marred occasionally by excessive gestures from Vince Wilburn jr's electronic Simmons drums. Unfortunately, the sound proved to be too unique for Columbia executives, who shelved the record for nearly four years. When *Aura* was eventually issued towards the end of 1989, Miles Davis was already a Warner Bros artist.

Some of Columbia's hesitation may be explained by the knowledge that Miles was negotiating a new contract elsewhere, and that with a solid-selling back catalogue it was pointless to invest further in an artist who was moving on. Miles had returned to live playing largely for financial reasons - the excesses of his retirement years, together with alimony and maintenance payments, had eaten into his resources - and he was increasingly aware that Columbia were putting much of their embattled jazz budget behind rising trumpet star Wynton Marsalis, with whom Miles had a complex relationship. Most notoriously, on June 28 1986 in Vancouver, Miles told his musicians to stop playing when Marsalis walked on-stage to sit in on a concert. It was a calculated snub that subsequently sharpened the younger man's contempt for Miles's "betrayal" of jazz, but it was also a double-edged gesture. Sitting in is an accepted part of jazz etiquette and Marsalis was already a star of some magnitude; some suspected that Miles was simply afraid of being outshone by a better technician with a parallel career as a much-admired classical soloist.

Star People, Decoy and *You're Under Arrest* were Miles's last three records for Columbia, and marked the end of his long association with the label, and with Teo Macero. Though his relationship with George Butler was of shorter standing, it was no less loyal on the company vice-president's part, even though he had become identified as Marsalis's champion; Butler expended some energy trying to make friends of the two trumpeters. Personal animosities aside, Marsalis's artistic reservations would only have been heightened by those final Columbia records. All are in the sharp electric funk mode that had become - ironically- Miles's longest lasting idiom. Miles's music and

Miles photographed at a press conference in his hotel in Nice. 1986

presentation were polar opposites to Marsalis's acoustic traditionalism and conservative manner. Marsalis's crisp suits and ties were 1950s jazz uniform; Miles appears on the cover of *You're Under Arrest* wearing expensive leathers, glowering out from under the brim of a similar fedora to the one worn on the more sober, monochrome cover of *Decoy,* and clutching a toy gun. It's an image that offers a strange, mixed message.

Released in the spring of 1983, *Star People* marked the first highpoint of Miles's comeback period. It also marked two different kinds of debut for Miles himself, and two farewells. The album's cover art, spare images of elongated human forms etched in crayon and Magic Marker, was the public beginning of Miles's second career, as a visual artist. A large and valuable proportion of his physical legacy on his death eight years later consisted of drawings and paintings which rapidly acquired high gallery prices for his estate. For much of his final decade, Miles drew almost obsessively, passing time in airports and dressing rooms filling sketchpads with abstract forms and with human figures which owed something to Picasso, something to Picasso's roots in African art, and something to Mati Klarwein. What began (on Cicely Tyson's suggestion) as therapy following a stroke in 1982 became a means of relaxation and a genuine mode of expression. It also sadly but inevitably fuelled detractors' claims that Miles had abandoned jazz for other pursuits.

Star People is also unusual in that Miles plays all the keyboard roles, something he had done intermittently since 1972 but never before to this extent. A new generation of electronic instruments offered polyphonic sounds, rich textures or percussive attacks, everything, in fact, he used to rely on Gil Evans to provide or Teo Macero to create in post-production. It's no coincidence that this was to be the last occasion on which Miles worked creatively with his two closest collaborators. Evans's great gift to modern jazz was that he saw no sharp divide between improvisation and composition. While preparing for *Star People*, he would record and transcribe rehearsal sessions, take melody lines from solos (most often guitarist John Scofield's) and shape them into new themes. As before, Macero shaped the music in the editing room, often bowing to Miles's wishes as he did when he grafted a short keyboard and guitar interlude onto the front of the title track.

Though Scofield played a role in creating the music on *Star People*, it was the often troubled Mike Stern who played on most of the album, a more straightforward, less "out" musician than his fellow-guitarist. The two guitarists appear together on "Speak", recorded in Houston, Texas, and one of two live concert cuts on the album. Paul Tingen calls the music of *Star People* "chromatic funk", a vivid description of Miles's current liking for showers of notes played over a solid beat. However frustrated he may have been with the style, Al Foster provided a solid foundation, his part coloured by extra percussion from Mino Cinelu. Except on "Speak", which features the young Tom Barney, Marcus Miller is the bassist. Bill Evans plays tenor saxophone on the title track, mostly soprano elsewhere, and is absent on "Come Get It", though one suspects that his importance to Miles was as much personal as musical. Certainly, he is featured much less than Kenny Garrett was to be later in the decade and often sounds the victim of abrupt editing.

At just under an hour, *Star People* is the longest album of Miles's final period. *Decoy* lasts under forty minutes, *You're Under Arrest* and *Tutu* just forty-two. Only *Aura* has greater duration and substance. In the summer of 1982 Miles was regaining strength and flexibility in his fingers following his stroke. By August he was playing with power and authority and a concert recording from Jones Beach Theatre, Long Island, of "Come Get It", which had replaced "Back Street Betty" as curtain raiser, is included on the album. As on *Live-Evil,* he was keen to mix concert tapes with studio material, and to blend live-in-the-studio immediacy with work that was much more obviously an engineering artefact. It is clear that "Star On Cicely" has been subjected to editing; it starts strangely and seems abrupt at just four and a half minutes. This, though, was a composition, apparently derived from a Mike Stern solo, that would continue to yield ideas for some years. Just as in bebop days, many "new" compositions were variations or "contrefacts" on standard songs, so in Miles's final years ideas appear and re-appear in different guises. The blues-based title track was reinvented as "New Blues", which later became a staple of Miles concerts. The original version ends poignantly. There are many moments in Miles's discography when he can be heard talking to his engineer, but the quiet "*Teo*" at the end of "Star People" sound like a farewell and the end of an era.

It wasn't quite the end of Miles's Columbia era. *Decoy* followed, an unsatisfactory record of mechanical funk made in the wake of his separation from Cicely Tyson, and made without the generative spark and steadying hand provided by Evans and Macero. Tunes like "Freaky Deaky" and "Robot 415" scarcely seem to belong on a Miles Davis record, even a record that is obviously in search of a new direction. Miles had recruited bassist Darryl Jones (now with the Rolling Stones) in place of Miller and in the course of the *Decoy* sessions replaced Bill Evans, who's only heard on the live "What It Is". The new soprano saxophonist, ironically, was

Branford Marsalis, elder brother of the man who would be cast as Miles's antagonist later in the decade. To fill the gap left by Macero, Miles enlisted the production help of Robert Irving III, who in turn acknowledged an ongoing debt to Gil Evans, hence the polite credit on "That's Right", though Evans had no direct role in writing or making the track. Irving is the credited composer on "Decoy" itself, which is the album's other highpoint. Once again, Miles showed that among his strengths were an ability to delegate some areas of creative responsibility while defending his own core conception. "That's Right" goes right to the heart of the blues, the source of Miles's most distinctive work.

If *Decoy* was patchy and unresolved, *You're Under Arrest* was more entertaining and, thanks to the pop visibility of "Human Nature" and "Time After Time" more commercially astute. According to Stuart Nicholson, *You're Under Arrest* "seemed to define Davis in the 1980s as *Bitches Brew* had in the 1970s and *My Funny Valentine* in the 1960s". That is a fair summing up, though the comparison with *My Funny Valentine* is apter in that *You're Under Arrest* broke no new ground but marketed a consolidating style. It's an eclectic record in the best sense, blending together hard funk tunes like the title track and "Katia" (named after John McLaughlin's pianist partner Katia Labeque), pop ballads, and in "Ms Morrisine" a fresh awareness of new influences, in this case reggae.

Miles also reprised "Jean-Pierre", but this time medleyed in an interesting new context. One of the striking things about the album, issued at a time when rap and hip-hop were exploring social agenda, is that it has a strong political colouration. Miles insisted that the record's full title is as it was printed in multiple scripts on the cover, *You're Under Arrest, You Have the Right to Make One Phone Call or Remain Silent, So You Better Shut Up.* He suggested that its informing spirit wasn't merely an African-American's reaction to police harassment - which had touched Miles more than once in his career - but a kind of spiritual dread that embraced political disenfranchisment, nuclear and environmental threat, as well as other philosophical issues. The tone of the record, that apocalyptic programme notwithstanding, is rather more satirical. "One Phone Call/Street Scenes"

Miles Davis with film director Spike Lee at the premier of Jungle Fever

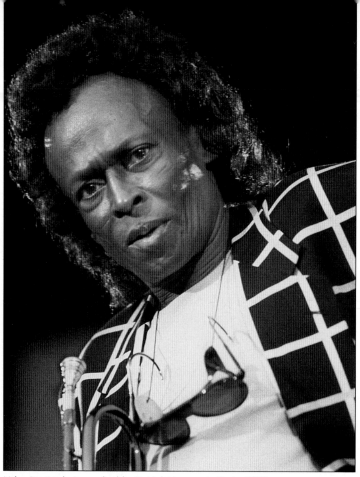

Miles Davis photographed by Patrick Hertzog in Paris. 1991

features spoken parts, Miles in bleakly comic mode accompanied by a series of guest "policemen", percussionist Steve Thornton, promoter Marek Olko (who was trying to persuade Miles to visit Poland) and rock star Sting, who like so many past guests just happened to be in the studio. The irony of his presence is that Branford Marsalis had declined a permanent place in Miles's group in favour of working with Sting's group. Marsalis's replacement was Bob Berg, a fine tenor and soprano saxophonist. It was still relatively unusual to hear a tenor saxophone in Miles's group, but Berg, who died in a 2003 road accident, is only sparingly used on *You're Under Arrest,* his solo on the title track heavily edited.

He also appears on a short strange medley, unique in Miles's canon, which brings together "Jean-Pierre", the theme to "You're Under Arrest" and a short piece called "Then There Were None", which begins with a tiny, delicate theme played by Irving on celesta and then has Miles's trumpet mimic a crying baby over synthesizer sounds intended to evoke nuclear warfare and civil collapse. Nowhere else in his career - not on *Jack Johnson,* not on the titling of *Tutu* or *Amandla* later - was Miles ever so overtly political or programmatic. There is no doubting its sincerity - the vision squares exactly with comments made in private over many years - but it was shrewd to include such a piece at a time of renewed political protest against the gung-ho foreign policy of President Ronald Reagan and Prime Minister Margaret Thatcher. Juxtaposed with the balladry of "Human Nature" and "Time After Time", both of which evolved into signature performance pieces, guaranteed *You're Under Arrest* and subsequent tours a growing audience.

Miles had never been more marketable and was thus in a strong position to renegotiate his contract. He was, however, increasingly uneasy at Columbia. Wynton Marsalis was the new house favourite, *Aura* had been shelved, and, for all Miles's efforts to reposition himself as a popular artist, he was still perceived as a jazz act and thus consigned to a receding corner of the budgeting process, and once again competing for advances with Marsalis. It was nonetheless a shock when in 1985 Miles severed a 30-year relationship and signed to Warner Bros. The move helped to secure him financially. It also put him close to Prince, the maverick young star who at the age of 19 had demanded and obtained total artistic freedom from Warners, repaying the debt by delivering *Purple Rain*, the album and associated movie that became an industry phenomenon, bridging a gap between white pop and black R&B and soul, and thus bringing together two previously irreconcilable musical audiences. Miles admired Prince's music, as he had once admired Sly Stone's, and admired his ability to play all the musical parts on his records. He also empathised with Prince's intensely private nature, the flipside to his flamboyant stage manner. The two men - aged almost 60 and 26 respectively - became friends, and Miles decided to record some of Prince's songs - "Penetration", "Jailbait", "A Girl and her Puppy" - but, as with a projected recording with Jimi Hendrix fifteen years earlier, plans for a full-scale collaboration were abortive. Prince sent Miles tapes of a new song in vocal and instrumental versions and seems to have liked what Miles did with them. The track was slated for Miles's first Warners record, but Prince seems to have had a change of heart and withdrew the offer, saying his music wasn't strong enough. "Can I Play With U?" has only ever been released in bootleg versions.

Miles made a slow start to his Warners contract. The Prince song would have been on the *Rubberband* record, which like Prince's *The Black Album* became one of the legendary "lost" discs of the 1980s. *The Black Album* was subsequently issued a decade later. Miles's tapes still lie the vaults. Not until January 1986 did Miles produce releasable music for his new label. *Tutu* is a fine, evocative record, featuring some fine trumpet playing, but despite the characteristic sole credit on the cover, it is really a collaboration, with Miles overdubbing his parts to tapes performed - Prince-like - by co-producer and multi-instrumentalist Marcus Miller. Though "Backyard Ritual" was written by another of the producers, George Duke, and "Perfect Way" is a Scritti Politi song, Miller is responsible for all the other compositions. He also plays bass, soprano saxophone, bass clarinet, guitar, synthesizers and drums on the record. The only other musicians involved were synthesizer player Adam Holzman (on "Backyard Ritual"), Bernard Wright in a similar role (on "Tomaas" and "Don't Lose Your Mind"), drummer Omar Hakim (also on "Tomaas"), electric violinist Michal Urbaniak (on "Don't Lose Your Mind") and roles for percussionists Steve Reid and Paulinho DaCosta.

The record was produced overall by Warners' Tommy LiPuma, a veteran in the business who may have lacked Teo Macero's creative genius but had a valuable foothold in pop and soul music as well as jazz. *Tutu* still sounds vividly contemporary, with a creative use of samples and modern dance beats. It is also deceptively subtle. "Tomaas" is a collage of melodic ideas that belies its initial straightforward impact. The presence of soprano saxophone and bass clarinet allies it to Miles's late 1960s experiments.

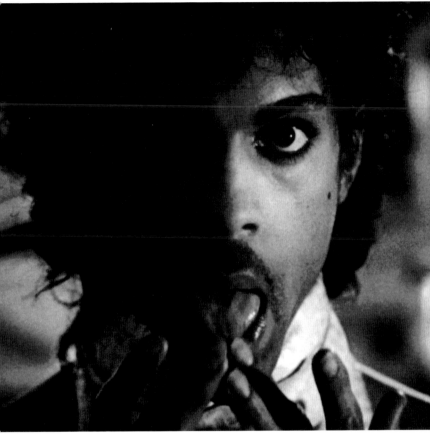

Prince in a portrait taken from his film Purple Rain. 1984

There were other echos of the past as well. The Spanish cast of "Portia" is reminiscent of earlier work with Gil Evans, while "Tutu" itself carefully interweaves rhythmic features from classic jazz, swing, and bebop as well as funk and soul. Miles's playing is mostly restrained, but when he raises the dynamics and intensity (as again on "Tomaas") it is clear that he is in very good lip.

The album's original title was to be *Perfect Way,* but LiPuma thought that "Tutu" was the strongest track of the session. In addition, Miles had become more actively involved with anti-apartheid activity, recording

Bishop Desmond Tutu during the 'Free Nelson Mandela' campaign. 1981

parts for a collective album by Artists United Against Apartheid called *Sun City* which had featured vocal samples by Bishop Desmond Tutu and Nelson Mandela. In 1989, he told a French interviewer that he would go to South Africa to "play for Bishop Tutu but I'm not going to play for the prejudiced white people . . . racists . . . I wouldn't be able to play one note". The fact that the situation was not "cool" in South Africa until after Miles's death meant that there was to be nothing in Cape Town or Johannesburg like the remarkable, liberating appearance in Warsaw in October 1986. On the cover of *Tutu* Miles has an iconic presence, almost like the two South Africans he so much admired. The record itself makes a second subtle reference to the apartheid struggle in "Full Nelson", though this is also a reference to "Half Nelson", the bebop tune Miles recorded on his debut recording as leader on August 14 1947. Even as he looked out to the wider world and namechecked an admired young contemporary (Prince Rogers Nelson), he was increasingly happy to revisit his own past.

Miles's next project was another collaboration with Miller, a soundtrack for the muddled thriller *Siesta*, directed by Mary Lambert (who had coincidentally been scheduled to direct Prince's second movie before he decided to do the job himself). Unlike the soundtracks for *L'Ascenseur pour l'echafaud* and *Jack Johnson,* neither *Siesta* nor the later *Dingo* sparked any new creative impulse in Miles. As he became increasingly willing to record advertising music, appear in promotional videos, and to make guest appearances on pop albums, so he seemed to approach soundtrack projects with the main aim of making money. Though his own albums were commercially successful and well received in the pop press, they were dismissed or reviled by most senior jazz critics. A review of *Tutu* in *The New Republic* stated flatly that "(Miles) has lost all interest in music of quality". It is a harsh assessment, but there is a context. The reviewer was Dr Stanley Crouch, a former drummer but now self-appointed guardian of traditional jazz values and tireless spokesman for Wynton Marsalis.

In June 1987, Miles began work on a new album that sounds programmatically like a companion piece to *Tutu*, but was actually a more accurate representation of what he was doing with his touring bands of the time. Even Miles aficionados have suggested that his official records of the 1980s were less significant than the growing row of concert bootlegs. Though *Amandla* - the Xhosa word for "authority" and a favourite greeting by African National Congress members - sounds like another political record, it is much more concerned with restoring some of the improvisational looseness that had disappeared with the final Columbia records.

On it, Miles introduced two players who would remain collaborators until the end of his life. Alto saxophonist Kenny Garrett had an intense, blues-based sound very different in timbre and tonality to that of the soprano and tenor players - Coltrane, Shorter, Evans, Berg - who had dominated his groups since the 1960s. Miles laughingly accused him of "wearing Sonny Stitt's dirty drawers", a reference which again suggested

Miles Davis and bass player Foley McCreary performing in Paris. 1990

he was revisiting the past. The other important new recruit was Joseph "Foley" McCreary, who had devised the concept of "lead bass", using a bass guitar as a front-line rather than rhythm section instrument. Miles's affectionate interaction with both men was a feature of most of his later concerts and both were given generous solo space.

One of the best tracks on *Amandla* was a tribute to an earlier "lead" bassist, Jaco Pastorius, whose spotlit improvisations had been a feature of Weather Report concerts. A victim of bipolar disorder, Pastorius declined into alcoholism and was beaten to death by a club doorman in September 1987, aged just 36. "Mr Pastorius" is *Amandla*'s highlight, marked by a plangent open horn solo from Miles, who may have been thinking less about the dead bassist on the piece - the tune and title were, once again,

Miller's - than about his old friend Gil Evans who had died peacefully in March 1988. An era was over.

Miles's own life had only three years to run. It is generally accepted that his final album, *Doo Bop*, issued posthumously in 1992 was a less than fitting memorial, an uneasy collaboration with rapper Easy Mo Bee. Its insufficiences have nothing to do with Miles's playing, which is again often very affecting, but with the basic incompatibility between hip-hop rhythms and Miles's unerasable jazz sensibility. More effective musical epitaphs were in the wings: a belated official live album from the final period, *Live Around the World*; complete reissues of the Blackhawk, *In A Silent Way*, *Biches Brew* and *Jack Johnson* sessions; an album of remixes from the electric period by bassist/producer Bill Laswell; various well-received exhibitions of artwork not shown in public during Miles's lifetime. There were signs, however, that the Miles Davis legacy would prove to be as cross-grained and intransigent as the man himself. A projected six-CD survey with remixes and unreleased material has had a chequered history, as if Miles had put a dead man's curse on the retrospective urge.

In the summer of 1991, Miles appeared at the Montreux Jazz Festival and with old friends at La Villette in Paris. Offstage he was frail, onstage commanding as ever. The French culture minister had made the one-time Prince of Darkness a Chevalier in the Legion d'Honneur, calling him "the Picasso of jazz" and praising his intransigent refusal to bow to any law but his own. He was, however, about to bow to a higher force, albeit on his own abrasive terms. The health problems he had been suffering that year were little different to those he had overcome in the past. Posthumous speculation suggested that Miles's Montreux and Paris appearances were calculated farewells. Posthumous rumours hinting that he had contracted HIV/AIDS, either from a shared needle or during a sexual encounter, were simply that, rumours sparked by the suddenness of his death and air of mystery surrounding it.

The real story, only revealed substantially later, has a familiar cast. In early September 1991, Miles had checked into St John's Hospital, near his West Coast home in Santa Monica, California, apparently for tests and monitoring. He was, however, suffering from the recurrent bronchial pneumonia that had afflicted him for many years. When it was suggested that a tracheal tube might relieve his breathing, Miles flew into a temper similar to the one that had caused post-operative damage to his vocal cords thirty years before. This time, though, the effect was more catastrophic. Miles suffered a major cerebral haemmorhage and lapsed into a coma. He survived some days before it was decided that his life-support system should be switched off. Miles Dewey Davis III died on September 28 1991. His body was transported across America, flying high over his native Illinois, and buried in Woodlawn Cemetery, not far from where Duke Ellington lay among his forebears. Two of America's greatest musicians were united in death.

Epilogue

The history of jazz in four words? "Louis Armstrong, Charlie Parker." Miles's assessment is not just incomplete but unduly modest. Add to that list the names of Jelly Roll Morton, who immodestly claimed to be jazz's inventor but was certainly its first great composer, and Duke Ellington, who raised jazz composition and orchestration to the status of art and who demonstrated an intuitive understanding of the proper balance between composition and improvisation, order and freedom, and you have a more rounded picture. Add the name of Miles Davis and the picture is almost complete, chronologically and creatively.

Charlie Parker's great recordings were made within a ten year span, but between Louis Armstrong's first mature recordings in 1925 and Miles Davis's last completely satisfying work in the mid 1980s most of the history of an entire musical form is bracketed, the short American century of jazz. Miles began his recording career working with an old blues singer and ended it working with young rappers. His earliest musical sensations may have been gospel choirs and field hollers in rural Arkansas, but he later admired Stockhausen, Cyndi Lauper and Prince. In between, he was present at the evolution of bebop, of "cool" and modal jazz, of a new kind of abstraction in jazz, and of jazz-rock, ending with a style that was completely and controversially *sui generis*. He was responsible for the greatest single change in the sound of jazz's signature instrument; trumpeters either sound like Louis Armstrong or, more frequently now, like Miles Davis. He exerts an influence on modern music that is so dominant as to be arguably pernicious.

The perceptive British writer Richard Cook has argued that it is time to set aside the Miles Davis legacy for the moment, declare a moratorium on tribute projects and albums, and allow the spotlight to fall on younger trumpet innovators like Terence Blanchard, Dave Douglas or even - and here Miles's ghost stirs restlessly - Wynton Marsalis. A similar stricture might apply to his former colleague John Coltrane and the tenor saxophone, a style so insidiously dominant that younger players are liable to be overlooked if they do not display some sign of a "Coltrane influence". And yet, unlike the majority of Trane disciples, those who have taken up Miles's challenge in a creative rather than nostalgic way have shown that it is, if not inexhaustible, then not yet exhausted. One thinks of artists as different as the American Wadada Leo Smith, whose Yo Miles project takes sustenance from some of the less admired areas of Miles Davis's career, the Pole Tomasz Stanko, whose "predatory lyricism" is a direct but individual offshoot of Miles's style, and the Austrian Franz Koglmann, who has developed his own version of Miles's death of jazz scenario to declare a new beginning for the music, as well as blending Miles's trumpet sound with that of Chet Baker, the "white Miles Davis".

It is in the nature of minor artists that they labour and labour with much noise and effort to produce a tit's egg, exquisite but exquisitely small. It is in the nature of bogus geniuses that they rumble and groan importantly like the mythical mountain, only to produce a mouse. It is the nature of very great geniuses that like active volcanos they dare to pour out vast amounts of smoke, vapour and sometimes sheer rubbish, but with it a core of magma that has the power to change cultural landscapes. Like Picasso, like Mailer and Stockhausen, Miles Davis chose to experiment and to experiment in public. His reputation for "taste" and delicacy has,

Towards the end, a portrait of Miles. 1990

like all generalisations about Miles Davis, to be balanced by its opposite. Much even of his officially released output was vulgar, unfinished and a creative dead-end. The privilege was to watch the process in the making, rather than its sanitised and edited retrospective version. The counter-counter-argument is that of all 20th century musical artists Miles was most dependent on the shaping and editing hand of collaborators, Gil Evans and Teo Macero most obviously, but also Marcus Miller later in his career. This is undeniable, but it was part of Miles's intuitive genius that he also allowed that process to be played out in public.

Like Mailer, Miles dared to take creative risks in public, often setting himself what seemed like self-defeating tasks, gestures of challenge and defiance toward the critical establishment. Inevitably, both have not just been misunderstood but pilloried and dismissed.

Miles Davis is one of the half dozen truly representative American musicians of the 20th century. Viewed from outside, his music may seem riven with contradictions, whether reversals of previous creative positions or apparent lapses of taste. Viewed from within, and in the context of a life and its times, it rather seems to embrace the contradictions of a country and a culture - freedom, racism, beauty, violence, nature, artifice, individuality, collectivity - and to express them with a remarkable singleness of purpose.

Other artists may have taken instrumental virtuosity to new heights. Miles never allowed technique to exceed what he had to say. Others may have taken a vernacular music and raised it to the level of art. Miles took a radically opposite view, taking an art form and ruthlessly stripping it back to its vernacular roots, in the process rescuing it from critical pigeonholing and bland commodification. His dismissal of the word "jazz" was at bottom a criticism of its grammatical use. Miles recognised that "jazz" is not a noun but a verb, not a reified form but an approach to music making that seeks to reconcile seemingly irreconcilable characteristics. They are the same ones listed above, the contradictions that cut deep fissures through American society and culture. Miles Davis made black music in a white culture, music whose axes were the most delicate beauty and the most scouring ugliness; he himself was a radical individualist who often chose to bury himself in the collective, or simply to absent himself from it for a while; a performing self who remained elusive and enigmatic; a man whose aesthetic seemed to assert both the perfect uselessness of art and its profound social function.

Change the focal length again and it might even be possible to reduce the names in that great tradition to one, and regard the music Miles Davis made between 1945 and 1991 as the perfect microcosm of one of the 20th century's great creative endeavours.

Year	Age	Life
1926		1926 Miles is born in Alton, Illinois on 26 May as the first son and second child of a dental surgeon, Dr Miles Dewey Davis Jr and Cleota Mae (Henry) Davis. Sister Dorothy born 1924 brother Vernon born 1929. The family moves to East St Louis shortly after Miles' birth
1939	13	Father buys him trumpet
1942	16	Starts to get jobs playing in local bars. Meets Irene Birth (Cawthon)
1943	17	Joined Eddie Randle's Blue Devils
1944	18	Just after graduating from high school he sits in with Dizzy Gillespie and Charlie Parker in Billy Eckstine's band. His father sends him to Juilliard School of Music in New York to study composition and piano. Birth of first child Cheryl to girlfriend Irene
1945	19	Abandons his academic studies for a full time career as a jazz musician, joining Benny Carter's band and making his first recordings (April or May). Records "Now's The Time" and other songs with Charlie Parker (November 26)
1946	20	Plays with Billy Eckstine in 1946-7. Birth of first son Gregory. downbeat magazine's "New Star on Trumpet"
1947	21	Member of Charlie Parker's group in 1947-8, making his recording debut as a leader on a session that featured Parker

Year	History	Culture
1926	Germany joins League of Nations. Hirohito becomes emperor of Japan. France establishes Republic of Lebanon. Antonio Gramsci imprisoned in Italy	Hemingway, *The Sun Also Rises*. A A Milne, *Winnie the Pooh*. Fritz Lang, *Metropolis*, T E Lawrence *The Seven Pillars of Wisdom*
1939	1 September: Germany invades Poland. Francisco Franco becomes dictator of Spain. Britain and France declare war on Germany	Steinbeck, *The Grapes of Wrath*. John Ford, *Stagecoach* (starring John Wayne). David O Selznick, *Gone with the Wind*
1942	Japan invades Burma; captures Singapore. German General Rommel takes Tobruk; battle of El Alamein	A. Camus, *L'Etranger*. Disney, *Bambi*. Popular Songs: 'The White Cliffs of Dover', 'White Christmas'
1943	Allies bomb Germany. Allies invade Italy: Mussolini deposed. Albert Hoffman discovers hallucinogenic properties of LSD	Rodgers and Hammerstein, *Oklahoma*. Sartre, *Being and Nothingness*. T S Eliot, *Four Quartets*
1944	Allies land in Normandy: Paris is liberated. Civil war in Greece	*Lay My Burden Down* (documentary about former slaves). Adorno and Horkheimer's essay on the 'Culture Industry'
1945	8 May: 'V E Day'. General election in Britain brings Labour landslide. 14 August: Japan surrenders, end of World War II	B. Britten, *Peter Grimes*. G. Orwell, *Animal Farm*. K. Popper, *The Open Society and Its Enemies*
1946	In Argentina, Juan Perón becomes president. In India, Bombay legally removes discrimination against "untouchables". In Britain, National Health Service founded. Winston Churchill makes 'Iron Curtain' speech	Bertrand Russell, *History of Western Philosophy*. Sartre, *Existentialism and Humanism*. Eugene O'Neill, *The Iceman Cometh*. Jean Cocteau, *La Belle et la Bête*
1947	Truman Doctrine: US promises economic and military aid to countries threatened by Soviet expansion plans. India becomes independent. Chuck Yeager breaks the sounds barrier	Tennessee Williams, *A Streetcar named Desire*. Albert Camus, *The Plague*. Anne Frank, *The Diary of Anne Frank*

Year	Age	Life
1948	22	Organises nine-piece band to play "cool" arrangements by John Lewis, Gerry Mulligan and others
1949	23	Recording contract with Capitol Records. In May, appearance at the Paris Jazz Festival
1950	24	Birth of second son, Miles IV. Little studio or live work. Death of Fats Navarro (July)
1951	25	Begins series of recordings for the Prestige label
1952	26	Records for Blue Note label
1954	28	Kicks drug habit. Further recordings for Prestige; first truly original work
1955	29	Appearance at the Newport Jazz Festival. Signs a contract with Columbia Records. Death of Charlie Parker (March 12) while Miles is in prison for non-payment of maintenance. Begins working with John Coltrane
1957	31	Capitol releases Birth of the Cool as LP. Records Miles Ahead for Columbia, first full-length collaboration with Gil Evans. Returns to Paris where he improvised film music for *L'Ascenseur pour l'Echafaud*. Permanently damages vocal chords after throat surgery
1958	32	Records *Milestones*. First professional contact with Teo Macero
1959	33	Records *Kind of Blue* (March 2, April 22) the most popular disc of his career. Beaten by police outside Birdland; charged with assault!
1960	34	*Sketches of Spain* (1959) wins a Grammy award. Married Frances Taylor (December). First significant symptoms of sickle-cell anaemia

Year	History	Culture
1948	Marshall plan (until 1951). Soviet blockade of Western sectors of Berlin: US and Britain organize airlift. In South Africa, Apartheid legislation passed. Gandhi is assassinated. State of Israel founded	Brecht, *The Caucasian Chalk Circle*. Greene, *The Heart of the Matter*. Norman Mailer, The *Naked and the Dead*. Alan Paton, *Cry, the Beloved Country*. Vittorio De Sica, *Bicycle Thieves*
1949	NATO formed. Republic of Ireland formed. Mao proclaims China a People's Republic	George Orwell, *1984*. Simone de Beauvoir, *The Second Sex*. Arthur Miller, *Death of a Salesman*
1950	Schuman Plan. Korean War begins. China conquers Tibet	In US, McCarthyism starts. Billy Wilder, *Sunset Boulevard*
1951	Anzus pact in Pacific	J D Salinger, *The Catcher in the Rye*
1952	Elizabeth II becomes Queen	Samuel Beckett *Waiting for Godot*
1954	Insurrection in Algeria. French withdrawal from Indochina: Ho Chi Minh forms government in North Vietnam	Kingsley Amis, *Lucky Jim*. J R R Tolkien, *The Lord of the Rings*. Bill Haley and the Comets, '*Rock Around the Clock*'
1955	West Germany joins NATO. Warsaw Pact formed	Tennessee Williams, *Cat on a Hot Tin Roof*. Vladimir Nabokov, *Lolita*
1957	Treaty of Rome: EEC formed. USSR launches Sputnik 1. Ghana becomes independent	The Academy excludes anyone on the Hollywood blacklist from consideration for Oscars (to 1959)
1958	Fifth French Republic; Charles De Gaulle becomes president. Great Leap Forward launched in China	Boris Pasternak, *Dr Zhivago*. Claude Lévi-Strauss, *Structural Anthropology*
1959	In US, Alaska and Hawaii are admitted to the union. Solomon Bandaranaike, PM of Ceylon (Sri Lanka), is assassinated	Berry Gordy founds Motown Records. Buddy Holly dies in plane crash. *Ben Hur* (dir. William Wyler). Günter Grass, *The Tin Drum*
1960	Vietnam War begins. OPEC formed. Oral contraceptives marketed	Fellini, *La Dolce Vita*. Alfred Hitchcock, *Psycho*

Year	Age	Life
1962	36	Three LP sets make it into the pop charts, including a live recording of a concert at Carnegie Hall, which is nominated for a Grammy. Death of Miles Davis II following level-crossing accident. First recordings with Wayne Shorter
1963	37	Tour of Europe
1964	38	Records *Four and More*. Death of Cleo Davis
1965	39	The second great Miles Davis Quintet embarks on a series of albums of original compositions contributed by the band members
1969	43	*Bitches Brew* (Grammy 1970) Divorces Betty Mabry. Narrowly avoids death when Ferrari fired upon by gangsters
1971	45	Birth of fourth and last child to Marguerite Eskridge. Erin becomes the only woman of Miles's children to work with him in music
1972	46	Breaks his ankles in a car accident
1975	49	Gives up recording due to illness. Undergoes surgery for a hip replacement
1980	54	Goes back to recording: *The Man With the Horn*

Year	History	Culture
1962	Cuban missile crisis. Jamaica, Trinidad and Tobago, and Uganda become independent. Satellite television launched	Edward Albee, *Who's Afraid of Virginia Woolf?* David Lean, *Lawrence of Arabia*
1963	J F Kennedy assassinated; Martin Luther King leads March on Washington. Kenya becomes independent. Organisation of African Unity formed	Betty Friedan, *The Feminine Mystique.* The Beatles, *'She Loves You'. Cleopatra* (Richard Burton and Elizabeth Taylor).Luchino Visconti, *The Leopard*
1964	Khruschev ousted by Leonid Brezhnev. First race relations act in Britain. Civil Rights Act in US. PLO formed. Word processor invented	Harnick (lyrics) and Bock (music) *Fiddler on the Roof.* Saul Bellow, *Herzog.* Stanley Kubrick, *Doctor Strangelove*
1965	Military coup in Indonesia	Neil Simon, *The Odd Couple*
1969	Neil Armstrong takes first moon walk. Internet created by US Department of Defence. Massive anti-war rallies in US	Mario Puzo, *The Godfather. Easy Rider* (Dennis Hopper and Peter Fonda). *Midnight Cowboy* becomes first wide-released X-rated film
1971	Nixon proclaims end of US offensive role in Vietnam War	Dmitri Shostakovich, *Symphony No. 15.* Solzhenitsyn, August 1914
1972	In US, Watergate scandal. Bloody Sunday massacre (N Ireland). Allende overthrown in Chile; Pinochet takes power. World Trade Centre completed. Optical fibre is invented	Richard Adams, *Watership Down.* Bertolucci, *Last Tango in Paris.* Francis Ford Coppola, *The Godfather*
1975	Franco dies; King Juan Carlos restored in Spain. Angola and Mozambique become independent. End of Vietnam War. Khmer Rouge seize power in Cambodia.	Boulez, *Rituel in memoriam Bruno Maderna.* Queen, *'Bohemian Rhapsody'*; first major rock video. Steven Spielberg, *Jaws*
1980	Indira Gandhi's Congress Party wins the Indian election; later her son Sanjay is killed in a plane crash. Soviet forces engaged in fierce clashes with Afghan Mujaheddin	Jean Paul Sartre dies. Henry Miller dies. John Le Carré, *Smiley's People.* Sir Cecil Beaton dies. Peter Sellers dies. John Lennon is shot dead in New York

Year	Age	Life
1981	55	Back on tour.Marries Cicely Tyson (Thanksgiving Day)
1982	56	Suffers stroke (January). Wins another Grammy for *We Want Miles*
1984	58	Meets artist Jo Gelbard, who becomes his art teacher, collaborator and lover
1986	60	After 30 years with Columbia Miles switches to Warner Bros. Records and released *Tutu*, which won him another Grammy
1988	62	Is award the final of his 23 Grammies for *Music from siesta*
1991	65	In July, Miles joins an orchestra led by Quincy Jones at the Montreux Jazz Festival. Dies on 28 September

Picture sources

The author and publishers wish to express their thanks to the following sources
of illustrative material and/or permission to reproduce it. They will make proper
acknowledgements in future editions in the event that any omissions have occurred.
Getty Images: pp. 7, 16, 32, 53, 72, 74, 76, 78, 83, 86, 100, 103, 119. 126,
133; Topham Picturepoint: pp. 10, 15, 18, 43, 44, 46, 49, 55, 57, 58, 61,
66, 68, 84, 88, 92, 108, 110, 112, 115, 123.

Year	History	Culture
1981	Greece becomes the 10th member of the European Community. Ronald Reagan is inaugurated the 40th President of the USA. First space shuttle 'Columbia' makes maiden flight	MOMA, New York, donates Picasso's *Guernica* to the Prado Museum, Madrid. Nobel Prize for Literature: Elias Canetti. Salman Rushdie: *Midnight's Children* wins the Booker Prize
1982	Argentinian forces invade the Falkland Islands (Malvinas); the UK sends task force, which land 21 May; Argentinian occupying forces surrender 14 June	*USA Today* published for the first time. Nobel Prize for Literature: Gabriel Garcia Márquez. Vietnam Veterans' War Memorial is dedicated in Washington
1984	Indian PM Indira Gandhi is assassinated by her bodyguard	Band Aid launches *'Do They Know It's Christmas?'*
1986	Portugal and Spain enter the European Community. President Marcos tries to cling on to power by rigging Philippine elections; fleas the country; real winner, Corazon Aquino succeeds him	Simone de Beauvoir dies. Rupert Murdoch's News International move *The Times* from Fleet Street to Wapping despite union strike action. Manet's *La Rue Mosnier aux Paviers* is auctioned for $12 million
1988	Soviet troops begin withdrawal from Afghanistan; Mikhail Gorbachev is elected President of the USSR. Zia ul-Haq is killed in plane crash; Benazir Bhutto wins election in Pakistan	Gabriel Garcia Márquez, *Love in the Time of Cholera*. Salman Rushdie, *The Satanic Verses*. *The Last Temptation of Christ* (director, Martin Scorsese)
1991	US-led coalition commences 'Operation Desert Storm' to liberate Kuwait from Iraqi occupation	Nirvana, *Nevermind* – emergence of grunge music from Seattle, USA. Alan Bennett, *The Madness of George III*. *Thelma and Louise* (director, Ridley Scott)

Acknowledgements

Writers don't always incur debts, but books invariably do. Grateful thanks to all those who previously wrote about Miles Davis, especially Jack Chambers, Bill Cole, George Cole, Jan Lohmann, Barry McRae, Eric Nisenson, John Szwed, Paul Tingen, and above all the doyen of Miles biographers, trumpeter Ian Carr, who has occasionally suspected me trying to do down Miles the man, if not the music. Their work - Chambers' *Milestones,* Bill Cole's *The Early Years* (NY, 1995), George Cole's *The Last Miles* (London, 2005), Lohmann's painstaking discography (Copenhagen, 1992), McRae's short but perceptive life (London, 1988), Nisenson's *'Round About Midnight* (NY, revised 1996), Szwed's *So What* (London, 2002), Tingen's *Miles Beyond* (NY, 2001), and Carr's definitive biography (revised, London, 1998) - are all required reading. Gary Carner's *The Miles Davis Companion* (NY 1996), Stuart Nicholson's *Jazz Rock: A History* (Edinburgh, 1997), Stephanie Stein Crease's *Gil Evans Out of the Cool* (Chicago, 2002) and Larry Hicock's *Castles Made of Sound: The Story of Gil Evans* (NY 2002) were also invaluable. Miles's own *The Autobiography* (London, 1990), transcribed, edited or ghostwritten by Quincy Troupe, is entertaining and often vivid, but should be treated with caution on matters of fact and should you want to hang on to some warm feelings about Miles himself; feminists should avoid it altogether.

This book happily acknowledges these debts; this writer a few more personal ones. Richard Cook, my co-author on now eight editions of *The Penguin Guide to Jazz on CD* (1992-2006), has been a constant friend and inspiration. He has rugged views about the nostalgic fetishization of Miles Davis and his work, and I cheerfully anticipate a generously impatient reaction to these pages. My elder daughter Fiona incurred her music teacher's wrath (and her father's pride) by playing her trumpet with the bell three inches off the floor, "just like Miles". Her sister Alice, who has her own unique perspective on these things, always loved the grooves and the cover to the unloved *On The Corner*, and that puts her ahead of the revisionist game. Now their brother John is being weaned on the same musical diet, though we suspect percussion may be his forte. And then there is wise, constant Sarah, who came along just on cue at the fag-end of the "dark period" and has ever since had to put up with endlessly re-cued records, Milesian tantrums over abandoned drafts, deep glooms when I fall too far behind the beat, but who keeps coming back . . . time after time.

BM

Song Index

General Index